FROM COUCH TO COMMUNITY
Activating the Potential of Small Groups

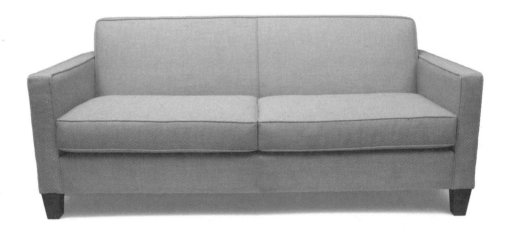

Loveland, CO

Group
Real. **Bold.** Love.

FROM COUCH TO COMMUNITY:
Activating the Potential of Small Groups

Copyright © 2014 Austin Maxheimer and Zach Below

Visit our website for more small group and church leadership resources: **group.com**

Credits

Authors: Austin Maxheimer and Zach Below

Editors: Bob D'Ambrosio and Amy Nappa

Assistant Editor: Kelsey Perry

Designer: Andy Towler

Unless otherwise indicated, all Scripture quotations are taken from the *Holy Bible*, New Living Translation, copyright © 1996, 2004, 2007. Used by permission of Tyndale House Publishers, Inc., Carol Stream, Illinois 60188. All rights reserved.

Library of Congress Cataloging-in-Publication Data

Maxheimer, Austin, 1981-
  From couch to community : activating the potential of small groups /
[authors, Austin Maxheimer and Zach Below]. -- First American Paperback.
     pages cm
  ISBN 978-1-4707-0962-4 (pbk. : alk. paper) 1. Church group work.
2. Small groups--Religious aspects--Christianity. I. Title.
  BV652.2.M35 2014
  253'.7--dc23
                                            2013047279

10 9 8 7 6 5 4 3 2 1   23 22 21 20 19 18 17 16 15 14

Printed in the United States of America.

CONTENTS

INTRODUCTION

Cultural Cows

Not long ago, I was headed to my grandmother's house when, out of the corner of my eye, I spotted a herd of cows. I remember asking my wife, "When did those get there?" Over the years I have driven that road hundreds, maybe even thousands, of times, and I had never noticed the cows before. Yet there they were, fat and motionless. I asked my grandma about them, and she told me they'd been there my whole life.

That's the thing about cows; they are inconspicuous. They sort of blend into the landscape without drawing attention. A grazing cow is boring, lifeless, and easy to ignore. Even though they are living, breathing, sentient beings, they seem more like a part of the scenery.

The world is filled with "cultural cows": ideas, practices, and philosophies in our culture that simply become part of the landscape and need to be inspected. If they go uninspected for too long, they become sacred cows. They turn into the things we dare not change for the sake of tradition.

For some sacred cows, the time has come to be slaughtered. Others simply need a prod to wake them up and get them moving. With the right prodding, a cow is a far cry from being boring, lifeless, and easy to ignore. All of a sudden, it is 1,000 pounds of powerful energy and a force that demands attention.

This book aims to do just that with small groups. We propose to actually stop the car, get out, and give the cow a prod.

Our argument is simple: Because small groups are typically understood and replicated as a model throughout American churches, they are a cultural cow worth inspection. The classic image of a small group that we all conjure up—8 to 12 Christians sitting in a circle in a living room with Bibles open ready for discussion, preceded by fellowship and followed by prayer requests—is something that needs to be reexamined. Prodded, if you will.

When it comes to church practices, taking a closer look can be a touchy endeavor as many of those practices have become sacred cows. We are also keenly aware that practices become "sacred" for a reason. Many people's experiences with small groups have been overwhelmingly positive and an essential part of their faith journey. Indeed, that is our experience as well. It is precisely because we love small groups and believe in the power of Christian community that we felt the need to write this book.

The Breakdown

The first part of this book is an honest look into the claims we make about small groups. If you've had any exposure to small groups, then you've heard words and phrases like "authentic," "accountability," and "life together" thrown around to describe them. What we want to ask is this: Are these descriptors truly valid? Should these words even be the pursuit of groups? Why are they championed in groups in the first place?

Part Two moves toward a solution. In order for groups to stamp "truth" on their claims and reach their full potential, we believe three fundamental shifts need to occur. The larger culture itself has shifted, and our expressions of smaller Christian communities need to evolve with it.

Part Three concludes with a call to action. This book is more a conversation and exhortation than it is a reflection on what our church has accomplished. However, we believe now is the time to act. Small groups have gone viral across the nation and are lying in wait for their unlimited potential to be unleashed.

We are very aware of the fact that not all small group ministries could or even should look the same. Your church may not even have small groups. Yet we do hold to a universal truth that Christians should live in community, and our argument is that those communities need to be activated.

Quick Housekeeping

Nobody enjoys minutiae or dry explanations, but we need to give clarity to just a few things:

Co-Writers: You may have noticed all the "we" talk here in the introduction. We are Austin and Zach. I (Austin) am the life group director for the One Life Network. Zach is a songwriter/worship leader/ordained minister/renaissance man. If you care to know more about us and this project, you can visit our blog at culturalcows.com and follow us on all those social media sites people use nowadays.

 As you read this book, you'll need to know that most chapters were written by one of us. We put the name of the author under the title of each chapter so you don't get confused when we use first person pronouns (like "I," for all you English flunkies). The few chapters that were co-written, well, you'll just have to figure that out on your own. In addition, if you see a sentence or thought underlined with a "thumbs up" symbol, it's because something Zach said stood out to me (Austin), or something I said stood out to Zach.

The Perfect Group: During the first draft of the book, we noticed we were constantly apologizing—saying things like, "We know there are good groups out there," or "Maybe this wasn't your group experience." Well, we decided to just apologize up front and be done with it. We know that many small groups are the most awesome thing since sliced bread. If this is your group, please don't take offense. Even if you have the most dynamic, awe-inspiring group of all time and you don't think you would change a thing about it, I guarantee you there is still something in here that will challenge and push you.

Culture: We talk a lot about culture in this book. Especially during the second half, in which we propose the three shifts small groups need to take in order to better engage our culture. Our simple definition for culture is "a shared set of beliefs, attitudes, values, practices, and behaviors." It's what we all experience together. One thing we want to be very clear about is that "culture" is not the enemy. Just because we are separating out what the church does and what culture is saying does not mean we are demonizing culture.

Let's Get Started!

What we hope comes across more than anything is that we love the church and truly believe it is God's redemptive plan for the world. That we naively and idealistically believe what the Bible says—that where there is light there can be no darkness; where the church is the kingdom of God should reign. That smaller groups of Christ-followers living in Christ-centered communities have the highest potential for reaching into the darkest places in our world and bringing the light of the Gospel into the lives of real people.

Chapter 1

IS THIS IT?
BY AUSTIN

Poetic Wax

Big or defining moments in life only become big or defining based on the effect they have on the life that follows. The actual moments themselves are simply singular events that lay no claim to the reverberations that ripple out and alter the courses of our lives.

If that seems a bit deep for a book on small groups, I apologize. I tend to get reflective and want to wax poetic anytime I think back on days or events or moments that seem so inconsequential while you are living them out; yet, when you look back and see the impact those events have had, you realize they literally changed the direction of your life. Irrevocably so in some cases.

Like sitting through a freshman college orientation or receiving a phone call while doing laundry. Not exactly world changers, right? Pretty mundane and routine even. Add in the fact that these were the two moments when I first met and then 5 years later reconnected with the woman who is now my wife, and they become big and defining moments. Sure, at the time they were exciting, pulse-racing, extremely emotional moments, but I've had plenty of those over the years. It was the *result* of each of those moments and the way they shaped my life that added to their meaning.

About halfway through my seminary experience, I had a moment that I now know has become a big, defining force in the direction of my life and that also happens to be the impetus behind this book.

God on the Golf Course

One weekend in seminary, two of my best friends came for a visit. I had lived life alongside these guys for years. All three of us went through middle school, high school, and college together. We remain good friends to this day. During their stay, we did what we do nowadays when we get together: play golf all day. Afterward, we went to a local pub, ate some food, had a couple drinks, and watched the game. It was a long, typical, good day.

Throughout the course of the day, we did what friends who rarely see each other do— we got caught up on each other's lives. We talked about work, family, and old friends, told funny stories, and reminisced. I also got to talk with them about God, Jesus, the church, and faith. I was, after all, in seminary, so these topics were very much just a part of the natural flow of our conversation. It wasn't preachy or alienating in any way. The conversation was simply borne out of our relationship and sharing what was happening in my life and what I was excited about.

There were a couple moments when it became more than just sharing, and some real dialogue opened up. I even remember one heated yet respectful discussion on gay marriage. I got to listen to their opinions, concerns, and frustrations with what they perceive as the typical Christian stance (as mostly understood through the conservative Christian right-wing political bloc). Then I got an opportunity to respond.

I don't know exactly what my two buddies believe about God, but I feel pretty safe in saying they would not describe themselves as Christ-followers. And I know that each of them hold a certain amount of hostility toward the church and the Bible. However, encouraged by the previous day's conversation and doing my due diligence as an evangelical Christian, I invited them to church on Sunday. I was pretty surprised when they actually showed up.

Wholly Unimpressed

 For some reason, Christians often hold to this mystical belief that if we can just get our friends into the church building, they will walk out forever changed. On one hand, that is absolutely ridiculous because it doesn't do justice to the long process of coming to faith that many of us go through. On the other hand, it is a kind of innocent naïveté. We want the people we love to experience what we are experiencing, and a Sunday morning church service is our best association for making that happen.

This is where my mind was on that fateful Sunday. I had been learning all this stuff in seminary that was revolutionizing my life. I was finding meaning and purpose and beauty in the Gospel and wanted to share that with two of my best friends, who had opened a door for me to do so.

When I met them in the parking lot, I immediately began seeing the day through their eyes. People do this all the time when going through an anticipated event they've invited others to join them in. When you are showing someone around your new home, taking friends from out of town out for a night in your city, or hosting guests at your kid's birthday party, your awareness of what other people are experiencing is heightened. You see familiar things in new and different ways.

My family loved that church. But as I saw that day through my friends' eyes, things looked very different indeed:

- They saw a bunch of strangers who probably smiled a bit too much.

- They were herded into a room and asked to sit, stand, sit, and stand.

- They watched some foreign "sacred" rituals.

- They heard songs that were a little cheesy, moderately performed, and in no way connected to them.

- They were talked *at* by a guy who they had never met and who had no real credibility with them.

- The message itself was not really directed to them but was more for the rest of the people in the room.

Then they shuffled out, largely unchanged and wholly unimpressed.

The Power of 52

It was in that moment that my understanding of church was forever altered. I always knew that church is the people, we are the church, and blah, blah, blah. However, it wasn't until that Sunday that I began to internalize that truth and live it out.

I wanted nothing more than my two friends to share in what I had been given and experience what I was experiencing. I saw that they were unable to connect with that gift and experience at a traditional Sunday morning church service in a building.

<u>That day the truth hit me in a powerful way. My friends experienced Jesus much more during our time together on Saturday than they did on Sunday.</u>

What's more, given their attitude and mindset toward Christianity and the church, even if they committed to attending 52 straight Sunday services (unless God went all Saul-on-the-road-to-Damascus on them) there would probably be nary a chink in their armor of unbelief.

However, transfer those same 52 experiences to interactions with people who actively and consistently live out their love for Jesus, and you might have a chance. Fifty-two times they would get to dialogue about faith questions—asking honest questions and receiving real answers. Fifty-two times they would see faith lived out in real and tangible ways. Fifty-two times they would experience countercultural sacrificial love. Fifty-two times they would get the opportunity to catch glimpses of Christ, instead of only seeing Christians. Fifty-two times they would build real relationships with people they could share their life with, instead of merely viewing the same spectacle. Fifty-two times they would witness something contrary to the negative perceptions surrounding Christianity.

> I love this. Notice how Austin didn't say that 52 small group meetings were the answer. It is relationally living out faith that makes the difference. We hold strong to the idea that this is what small groups *could* be.

Perception Problem

Let's just face the facts here—the church and Christianity have a major perception problem. A recent Gallup poll found that an all-time low 44 percent of Americans have confidence in the church.[1] People outside the church, who categorize themselves as non-Christians, called Christians hypocritical, anti-homosexual, sheltered, too political, and judgmental.[2] Nearly half of young Christians between the ages of 18 and 29 are leaving the church, claiming it is shallow, overprotective, anti-science, repressive, exclusive, and doubtless.[3]

Yet given all that data, there is one last number that creates a statistical conundrum: 77 percent of Americans still claim, to some degree, to be followers of Jesus Christ.[4]

These facts cannot coexist; they are illogically juxtaposed. Nearly 80 percent of Americans claim to follow Christ, but only half that number say they trust the church, the active body of Christ.

At the same time, people would not use the above laundry list of negative descriptors regarding Christians and the church in reference to their friends, family, neighbors, and co-workers who are in fact Christians. If everyone who was not a Christian or was leaving the church really thought the other 80 percent of Americans were shallow, anti-intellectual, overprotective, and insensitive, then we would probably have societal breakdown due to the esteem we hold for those around us.

So we know these very real negative perceptions are directed more toward a caricature of Christians and the church than they are toward the real people in our lives who we know, love, and respect. Nowhere is that caricature upheld more than at a traditional Sunday morning worship service, and at no time does it break down faster than when people start living life alongside each other.

> This is so true. I work at a fitness center. Many of the employees there hold hostility toward the church and Christians. They would use many of these same negative adjectives to describe Christians. At the same time, they know that I am a Christian and hold no hostility toward me. In fact, I am officiating the wedding of one of my co-workers who is anti-church but, I guess you could say, pro-Zach. Stereotypes break down in relationships.

Full Circle

And now we've fully circled around to the weekend with my two best friends those many years ago. My friends would not describe me as shallow, overprotective, anti-intellectual, judgmental, and the lot (at least I hope not!). Yet, I'm a Christian. And they know that.

As long as the emphasis remains on the deep bond of shared relationship and not on the negative perception of the Christian caricature, stereotypes break down. When we do normal, familiar activities, the wall that blocks the good news of Jesus Christ is not up. In fact, someone may even be able to truly experience Jesus. Or at least a few bricks might go missing from the normal wall that blocks the message, and some of it can leak through.

That was my first awakening of the weekend—I saw how smaller gatherings of Christ-centered communities could break through the negative perceptions people hold against Christians and the church. Dialogue and natural conversation could stand in place of speeches and being talked at. These smaller groups could easily meet people where they're at. Like the golf course. The ultimate goal being that we should create safe environments for people far from God to explore matters of faith that are both intellectually satisfying and experientially credible. But this was only the first step.

Is That It?

A second and much deeper discontent that weekend began to stir in me. I could almost hear my friends say at the conclusion of the service, "That's it!!??"

"This is what you are dedicating your life to? That's what all the hubbub is about? That's what you couldn't wait to get me to? That's the so-called God of the universe's plan for the world? That's the big reveal of the church?"

My two highly intelligent friends, giving them their due credit, could probably intuit that whatever was going on inside me was much deeper and more meaningful than what they had just experienced. And because of our relationship, they might even allow a shred of credence for it in my life. But why in the name of all that is holy would they care about it? If people just gather for an hour, hear some announcements, listen to some insider language, and poorly sing a few songs—why should they care? Why would they get involved? I'm sure they would much rather be a part of the "Watch Football and Golf When Football Is Not In Season Sunday Morning Club." By the way, if anyone starts that club, please let me know.

That is when my holy discontent became clearly defined: I wanted to devote my life to connecting people to the church and the church to the community. It is my conviction that without Christians gathering as the body of Christ to be present in our communities and affect real life change, the American church will slowly be sucked dry of its vitality and will eventually shrivel up to be a shell of the image we see in Scripture.

Lampstands

The biblical image of the church is that it is the hope of the world. There is this beautiful picture of the church in the opening scene of Revelation. The church is represented as lampstands throughout the world, and Jesus is walking among them in the fullness of his majesty, keeping them lit through the brilliance of his glory—giving life as he goes. Here are some biblical examples of the church being associated with light:

- Jesus, while teaching his followers how they should act in the world and be perceived by the world, calls them the light of the world—not to be hidden away, but to shine so brightly that men have to glorify God (Matthew 5:14-16).

- Paul, writing to the church in Ephesus, calls them children of light and says the fruit of light consists of all goodness, righteousness, and truth (Ephesians 5:8-9).

- In 1 John, the people of God (the church) are called the light of God, and where there is light, there can be no darkness.

Can we say those things about our churches? That in the communities where our churches are there is no darkness? That when people look at our churches they see Jesus Christ in all his splendor and majesty? That the fruit of our churches is goodness, righteousness, and truth? That because of the actions of our churches, people have no choice but to give God all the glory?

If we could answer in the affirmative to all these questions, I wouldn't have to worry about my two friends catching a glimpse of the beauty, meaning, and purpose that was transforming my life; it would simply radiate out from the brightness of the church's light. They would see and feel its impact.

And that is where small groups come into play. Even if you have one big, bright light shining in your city or community, there are still dark spots and shadows cast throughout it. But as small groups, which are really just mini-churches, grab hold of the mission of connecting the church to the community, lights begin to pop up that remove darkness even from the smallest nooks and crannies—places where the larger church body just cannot reach.

Small groups have the distinct advantage of being decentralized, inherently relational, and able to mobilize. With the emphasis on small groups over the past 30 years or so, the church is primed to usher in a fresh explosion of compassion through these groups. There are thousands upon thousands of mini-churches/mission teams poised to unleash the good news through word and action in our neighborhoods, communities, and cities. It is time for a big shift in the function and purpose of our small groups.

Part One:

THE CULTURAL COWS OF SMALL GROUPS

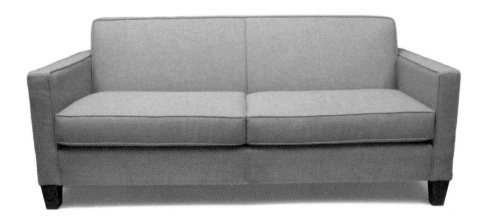

FROM COUCH TO COMMUNITY

Chapter 2

WHITE KNUCKLE GRIP

BY ZACH

Stirring

Perhaps you have the same stirring in your soul that Austin and I share; the deep feeling that somewhere at the core of this idea of relational community is the endless potential for affecting real change in our lives, churches, and cities. Along with that hope, you may also have the gut feeling that this potential is lying dormant, powerless and impotent, waiting to come alive.

White Knuckle Grip

Let's just put it all out there and start with the bad news. To say it nicely, small groups are missing something. To say it bluntly, they are failing.

You may be thinking, "That can't be right. Small groups have surged over the past 30 years." It's true. On some fronts small groups have been wildly successful. There are countless churches that have exploded with growth thanks to their small group ministry. When we zoom out and look at groups solely from the view of church growth and integration, it's a clear winner. As a result, the current model or expression as a whole remains fundamentally unexamined. Sure, there always has been and always will be an ongoing conversation about small groups. There is an overflow of books written, conferences attended, and resources available. Yet the majority of these materials are still written within the original framework that sprung up in the '80s.

So if groups are growing, how are they failing? They are failing on these two fronts:

1. Being mission driven.

2. Living up to their claims.

Mission Driven

The church as a whole has worked hard to clearly define its core mission: helping those far from God experience Jesus. While the church has zeroed in on its mission, groups have continued unchanged, having been given a free pass to operate outside the mission. They have become their own island, with their own government, rules, and laws.

The second half of this book speaks in detail to the remedies and relationship of small groups and mission. For now, ask yourself the following questions:

- When was the last time someone came to a saving relationship with Christ in your group or any group that you know?

- Or, more simply, look around your group. Is there anyone there who isn't already fully immersed in the church?

- Is there anyone there *because* they desperately need God?

- Does the outside world even know your group exists? Does the neighbor two houses down from where you meet know?

Living Up to the Claims

Beyond the huge issue of operating outside the church's mission, we still have to deal with groups in their current context. An oversimplified definition of the current context is a group of 8 to 12 people sitting in a circle in someone's living room for the purpose of fellowship, some form of study, and prayer. Usually in that order.

With that model in mind...

- Do we really believe that our groups, as they are currently expressed, are reaching their full potential?

- Do our groups offer purpose and value?

- On the practical side, are the words we throw around to describe small groups (discipleship, accountability, natural, inviting, authentic, life together, biblical) accurate? Or have we simply settled, ideologically abandoning groups to the land of business as usual?

We have to recognize where we are missing the mark before we can innovate new solutions and unleash the power of groups. Over the next few chapters, we'll take a deeper look at the current expression of small groups and bring to light what needs prodding.

The last thing we want to do is spew negativity about small groups. We fully believe that community is essential and absolutely necessary in the God-journey. It's because of that need and dormant power that we feel the need to restart the conversation. A conversation on what small groups *could* be. It's time to prod the cow.

My Small Groups Story

It seems appropriate to frame this discussion with the reality of what an outsider coming into a small group looks like. What it feels like. This is my story. A firsthand account of the difficulty and awkwardness of summoning the courage to join a small group.

I was born, raised, and fully integrated into all things church. I grew up a pastor's son. I attended a Christian college. After college I transitioned right into full-time ministry. If you're in full-time ministry, people go out of their way to get to know you. They send you cards, take you to lunch, bake you muffins.

For me, church was always comfortable. I knew everyone and everyone knew me, so small groups never raised any cautionary flags. My take was that everyone had the same experience I had. Small groups were easy and painless—so I thought.

Fast forward to age 26, my first year out of full-time ministry. My wife and I moved from our comfy church in east Tennessee to Illinois, so she could finish up her doctoral program. One year later we packed up the truck again and headed to Nashville, Tennessee.

One of the first things on our to-do list: find a church. We did some online research and found a large church we were excited about getting plugged into. We walked in on our first Sunday, and much to my surprise, no one was dying to meet me. There were no muffin baskets, no lunch invitations. Just the giant smiles of the greeters and the stark reality that we knew no one.

We decided to look into small groups. So we found the very prominent small groups booth and chatted with the lady behind the table. We filled out a little survey, signed up, and walked away excited about our first group in Nashville.

Then a month went by. We got an email every couple of weeks saying they were still looking for a group that would be a "good fit" for us. No problem. If we were really going to spend the foreseeable future doing life with this group, I appreciated their diligence in finding the right place for us. But the timeline kept extending.

> While some churches are undoubtedly better than others at moving newcomers into groups, I can guarantee that your church's connections process is broken. Any connection that is a "process" is inherently broken. What's worse, groups often use the church's connection process as a crutch and/or excuse for not pulling people in from their real lives and existing relationships. The only failsafe way to grow and multiply groups is for every person in every group to pull in people they actually know.

In month two, we got an email. It was an invite to a small groups open house. So on a Wednesday night, my wife and I left work early and rushed to church. We walked into the worship center, and it had been transformed. It was now set up in 30 or so circles of chairs.

We checked in, got name tags, and were told to "move around, join a circle, and jump in the conversation" to see if we connected with anyone. I was thinking, "Do what now?" I'll pause to let the immense awkwardness and extreme discomfort fall over you...

Nonetheless, like all good cattle we fell into the herd. Much to our surprise, we did connect with a few people. We went through the standard questions of "What do you do for a living? Where are you from? How long have you been at this church?" At some point without realizing it, we had transitioned into natural conversation. One of the guys was a musician; I was a musician—*check*. Another guy was a sports nut; I was a sports nut—*check*. They didn't have any kids; neither did we—*check*. They thought this whole process was crazy; so did we—*check!*

This group seemed like a great fit. We actually laid out a day of the week and time that worked for all of us. Looking back, this is where we should have exchanged info, walked out, and started meeting. Instead, one of the small group pastors came and took our information and told us she was excited to get us going "officially."

Within a few days we got a call that our group had been formed. That Sunday evening, after a two and a half month process, we were pulling into the driveway of the people the church hand-picked for us to share our lives with. I saw smoke from a grill. I smelled hamburgers. I was pumped.

When we knocked on the door, someone we had never met answered. They walked us to the back deck, and much to my surprise, I didn't recognize anyone. There wasn't a single person from the open house.

I struck up a conversation with the first guy. He loved working on cars. I can barely put gas in my car—*miss*. I asked another guy, "Did you see the UT game this weekend?" He answered, "I'm not really into sports"—*miss*. Next, a total of five kids went running through the backyard—*miss*.

We labored to find some common ground, and I'm sure we did. But I think everyone knew within the first meeting that we were not the right fit for that group. Instead of voicing our concern and trying to connect with another group, we stuck it out.

It was fine. Nothing more, nothing less. We never really looked forward to going, but we felt guilty if we skipped. We followed the standard small group format: fellowship, teaching, and prayer.

Each week we would share a meal together. This was the only natural part of the whole group time. We would actually hang out and talk about what was going on in our lives.

As the night moved closer and closer to the scheduled "discipleship" time, the room changed. I'm not kidding, it got weird! Someone would unenthusiastically say something like, "We should probably start the lesson now," to which everyone would shuffle into the living room and stare blankly at each other. We had just talked naturally for an hour, but when we moved into structured time, no one had anything to say.

Our group was made up of two couples with kids and two couples without kids (this included Jaime and I). Obviously, I was a little thrown when we began a study called *Raising Godly Children*. Especially considering the fact that one couple in our group had recently been told they could not conceive. Still, we spent our first 8 to 10 weeks studying (I say that very loosely) how to be godly parents and raise godly children.

Needless to say, the study had little lasting impact on my life. Even more, it was clear from the lack of preparation from the leaders (with kids) that it wasn't challenging them either. Most weeks we would rush through the material just to check it off our "small group checklist," and we would leave trying to think of an excuse to get out of the next week.

In the last 5 to 10 minutes of our time together, one of the leaders would ask for prayer requests. Again, an awkward silence would fall over the room. We would close in prayer, everyone would leave, and we'd do the same thing the following week.

No one ever invited anyone (thank God for that!), and no one spent extra time outside of group with one another. We were "living life together" for an hour and a half sharp once a week.

The Reality

Why does this matter? It matters because I can't stop thinking about the guys in Austin's story. I can't stop thinking about my friends who haven't experienced God yet. If our mission is to help people experience Jesus, then it has to be a stamp on everything we do.

I try to imagine what it would be like if my friends had lived through my small group experience. I think about what would happen if they joined the average small group in America. No matter how I spin it in my head, the alarming and sad truth is that if I actually talked them into coming to group, they would walk into a very awkward situation and likely never come back.

That fact alone is reason enough to loosen the white knuckle grip we have on the current expression of small groups. It's time to take off the wide zoom lens that we as the church have allowed small groups to operate under. Like gold, we must be refined by fire. We must allow that fire to bring the impurities to the top. So we begin with what has surfaced. The buzz words around the small groups world are words like life together, community, inviting, natural, and authentic. Are these accurate characteristics of life in a small group? The reality is—they're not. Not by a long shot.

Chapter 3

CULTURAL COW #1: ON MISSION

BY AUSTIN AND ZACH

On Mission?

Cow prodding takes courage. If we're going to get things moving, we have to examine the claims of small groups. We need to determine if they're what they claim to be or merely sacred cows resting in the pasture. So we begin our quest with the first cow: mission.

You don't need to go back and scan our list of buzzwords to see if mission was on there. It wasn't. Mission is not on the buzzword list because it is absent from the traditional small group paradigm. It's hard to believe that something the church gives so much time, energy, and resources to (small groups) would pass unfiltered through the mission of why the church exists in the first place. Thus, we feel it necessary to filter all our claims through the idea of mission.

You may be thinking, "Doesn't the church exist for multiple reasons?" Well, the answer is yes. You could argue that the church exists for fellowship, bringing like-minded people together, building up the saved, and many more reasons. These are all true and good. However, once you trim away the fat, the core mission is to bring people who are far from God into a saving relationship with Christ. This, above all else, is the church's foremost mission.

Starbucks Without Coffee

Not long ago, Bob, our CFO and elder, made his daily trip to Starbucks. He waited in line, scanned the menu, and prepared to order. Much to his surprise, the ever bubbly barista informed him that they were *out* of coffee. Yes, Starbucks, the embodiment of coffee, was out of coffee.

The tweet Bob posted that morning has stuck with me to this day. He said, "There's just something about stopping by Starbucks and they're out of coffee that seems off mission" (@BobSeymore).

It reminded me of the current dilemma within our small group culture. Starbucks' mission had not changed that morning, yet everyone would agree they missed the mark. In fact, that's why we respond to such an incident by saying, "Whaaat? Are you serious? There's no way that just happened." It's hard to imagine Starbucks minus the coffee. It's why they exist. Sure, they sell pastries and mugs and dabble in underground hipster CDs, but without coffee there is no Starbucks.

For the church, helping people far from God experience Jesus is "the coffee." Every other thing the church does (including small groups) is pastries, mugs, and CDs. People love Starbucks' pastries, but they go for the coffee.

Relentless Pursuit

I'm (Austin) the life group director (small groups pastor) at One Life Church. Our mission is stated as "Helping people far from God experience Jesus." Not exactly innovative or groundbreaking stuff. Seemingly every contemporary church that has a public mission statement talks about or uses some variant of this statement. As they should. I have heard our lead pastor ask relentlessly: "Are we on mission? Are we devoted to reaching unchurched, secular-minded people? Look at the service through the eyes of a guest, through the eyes of someone who is far from God or exploring Jesus—is the mission being met? Is the service for them; does it have them in mind? Are we on mission?"

As a lead team we revisit these questions regularly. If an area is missing the mark or failing altogether, we revise it and implement a new strategy or operating procedure.

It was One Life's relentless pursuit of being driven by mission that led me to sell out to the church and volunteer in life group leadership and eventually come on staff and remain excited to go to work every single day. But even though our church is mission driven, I have spent the first year and a half of my leadership capital trying to get our groups to see themselves not as a separate activity within the mission but as an essential part to the mission itself.

I have walked through this exercise with my leaders:

Connect to the Mission

1. Picture what happens at a typical small group.

2. Now picture an unchurched, secular-minded person. Create a profile based on real people you know and personal experience.

3. Would that unchurched, secular-minded person feel comfortable? Is that group something they'd want to be at? Something you'd want to invite your friends to?

4. How can your group create environments where people feel comfortable exploring God in ways that are credible to their lives experientially *and* intellectually? How can you help them truly experience Jesus?

The reason we have to walk through that exercise is because our groups are not on mission, at least not directly.

Mission Implications

We'll talk in great depth about getting groups on mission in Part Two. We'll address shifts that can transform our groups from a huddle of Christians to lampstands in our communities.

For now, we proceed to the remaining cultural cows. We'll examine the claims we make about small groups as they are currently expressed.

However, since being "on mission" affects every aspect of small group life, we've dedicated the last section of the next six chapters to the implications of our actions, or lack of action, on our mission. You'll know you are there when you see the heading *On Mission: For Group Discussion*. Consider using these questions for discussion with your small groups and leadership teams.

Chapter 4

CULTURAL COW #2: DISCIPLESHIP

BY ZACH

Sacred Cows and Church Droids

When you start messing around with the sacred cow of small groups, the first question you get is "What happens to discipleship?"

If you've been around the church world long, then just like a song that gets stuck in your head, the idea of discipleship at the forefront of small groups gets stamped on your brain. It gets cast as the anchor of small groups, and we unconsciously soak it all in. We've never really felt it necessary to examine the claim. At some point it was taught and it made sense, so we moved on.

So when Austin and I first started talking about a paradigm shift in small groups, like a good church droid I said, "What about discipleship? Aren't small groups designed to help those who already know God draw closer to him through discipleship?"

I'm not sure Austin knew the power of his next question or the effect it would have on both of us. It's a question we may not want to ask if we want small groups to simply keep growing unexamined. I could have remained happy in my ignorance. But like any good leader does, Austin answered me with one of those annoying questions that had to be dealt with. We had just met with our small group, and after a less than thrilling lesson, Austin, half exhausted and half frustrated, simply said, "Honestly, what would we be giving up?"

Austin's question set off one of those light bulb moments. Like glass, the unfound truths I held about the relationship between small groups and discipleship began to shatter around me. For the first time, I gave an honest look at our claims of discipleship. It didn't take long for the cultural cow of small group discipleship to peek its head out. It showed itself in three forms:

1. Small groups produce a flawed definition of discipleship.

2. Small groups give this definition of discipleship too much power.

3. Discipleship is not really happening in our groups.

Jedi Mind Tricks, Made Up Churches, and Discipleship

If I asked you what discipleship looked like in your small group, what would you say? Likewise, if I said that our small group was built around fellowship, discipleship, accountability, and prayer, would you immediately picture what each individual piece looks like? Where would your mind go?

I can tell you where my mind used to go. It went to the same place as 95 percent of the people I asked. Almost every person I talked with said that discipleship in small groups was the Bible study portion, lesson time, or teaching. What's truly interesting is that across the board they answered as if they knew it wasn't true but felt like they would get in trouble if they answered any other way.

Out of these discussions came the realization that small groups have led us to a pigeon-holed idea that is wide open and complex. It's as if some "small groups Jedi" had waived his hand and used a Jedi mind trick on us all: "These aren't the droids you're looking for. Discipleship in groups equals Bible study."

Our brains love it when difficult concepts have walls and boundaries. That's why we buy into articles like "Shed 10 Pounds in 6 Days" and "5 Steps to Earn More Money." We know there is no quick fix when it comes to health and fitness, but we love the idea that fitness is as easy as a 6-day commitment. Likewise, we know there are no lasting shortcuts to success, but the idea that we have control over the timeline is extremely appealing.

We are guilty of the same thinking when it comes to the idea of discipleship in the church, especially in small groups. We all know that discipleship is a lifelong journey to know God, but it feels much more attainable if we define it as an hour-long Bible study once a week. Allowing it to be anything more makes it messy, untrackable, and unorganized.

What's interesting is that I don't believe we are taught this verbally from our church leaders. Sure, the church's desire to be optimally organized and track member progress may fan the flame. Furthermore, programming study time gives church leaders the feeling that they have at least some control over the discipleship process. However, I don't think it's a conscious misleading. I maintain that there is not a church leader out there who would say Bible study is the totality of discipleship. Yet somehow, without realizing it, we compartmentalize our small groups to say just that. The first 20 minutes, when we eat snacks and chat, is fellowship. The 30 minute lesson that follows is discipleship. We close with a sharing/prayer time that we call accountability.

 The truth is, <u>if we believe that discipleship is what happens through a half hour study one day a week, our definition of discipleship is grossly incomplete.</u> We know there are endless ways to explore discipleship within our small groups. It's time we educate our people on what it really means to be a disciple of Christ and give our groups the freedom to explore the concept creatively.

Too Much Power

One of the natural consequences of allowing Bible study to parade around as our only method of discipleship in groups is that we give it too much power. If we believe that our study time really is our only means of discipleship in groups, then we have to make it the central piece of what we do. And that's exactly what we've done. We elevate the formal study time to the point where we allow it to hold our groups hostage. We feel limited in what we can do in our groups, because we are anchored down by this incomplete idea of discipleship. That's why when groups meet but plan on skipping the study, we advertise it as a "fellowship night."

Everybody Ought to Go to Sunday School, Sunday School, Sunday School

Part of the power we give formal study in groups probably stems from our own concessions throughout the progression of church. Without going into the long history of Sunday school, or the Education Act of 1879, let me just say that by the mid-20th century, Sunday schools were all the rage. You can do a quick Google search and find lithographs of Sunday schools dating all the way back to the 1930s. I even found antique "Perfect Sunday School Attendance" ribbons for sale online.

I believe that the phasing out of Sunday school had a major impact on the formation of small groups, especially in smaller churches. I can almost guarantee that if your pastor grew up in the church and is over the age of 30, Sunday school played a big part in his or her life. While the following story is theoretical—it is all too real.

Mainstream Church in Somewhere, USA

In 1965, the Williams, Adams, and Stewart families feel the call from God to plant a church. After months of fundraising and strategy meetings, Mainstream Church in Somewhere, USA is born.

Before you know it, their small church of 30 has grown to 50. Within a year or two they are at 100 members. They see lives being changed, and God is blessing their efforts. An integral piece of this growth is Sunday school—a place where anyone can come to study the Bible and learn what it means to be a follower of God. Like a CEO starting a business, Mainstream Church is their baby. They have prayed, cried, and sacrificed for it. And in their minds, each piece of the puzzle is crucial to its success.

Fast forward 30 years. Mainstream Church is still around and has grown to almost 400 people. Ministers have come and gone, leadership has changed multiple times, but the Williams, Adams, and Stewart families still faithfully attend. They have had the privilege of seeing multiple generations of families born and raised at Mainstream. Those who were in the nursery when the church began 30 years ago are now adult Sunday school teachers and elders. Their grandchildren are now coming up through the same Sunday school programs they started all those years ago.

So when a minister who has been there for two years suggests getting rid of the Sunday school program and replacing it with small groups, there is natural hesitation. The minister reassures the elders, who reassure the founding members, who reassure the Keenagers, who reassure the Wednesday Morning Hat Ladies, who reassure the Sunday school teachers, who reassure the nursery workers, who reassure the infants that small groups will look a lot like Sunday school but will meet at homes in the community. The minister says that people will be more authentic in homes, and groups will be more comfortable for people who might have adverse feelings about church.

> We probably need to clarify just a bit, because we believe that fundamentally the goal of Sunday school and small groups is the same: *make disciples.* However, it is the approach that creates the difference: Sunday school was enacted to intentionally teach biblical principles and doctrine to people already professing faith. Small groups were enacted so that people, regardless of belief or not, could interact with and see faith in action.

The elders agree that as long as discipleship and teaching are still an integral piece of these groups, they are on board. Concessions are made, and small groups are formed. Both sides feel like they've won, and two very different concepts (Sunday school and small groups) with different philosophies end up sharing the same foundation.

It Happens!

I have seen this example played out more than once. In fact, I have been present during similar conversations and similar situations. While I'm confident that Sunday school played a role in lifting the "study" piece of groups to such a high level, whether this is how it actually happens or not is a moot point. The point is that it happens! On a weekly basis, we elevate the study to the central portion of our groups and all other facets must be tucked in around it.

Let's finally break the chains and cry freedom. It's time to decentralize Bible study and allow our groups to explore God in new ways. I'm not saying we should get rid of Bible study in groups. I'm not even saying we shouldn't have some form of study every week. We simply cannot allow it to guide all we do when we know that study is not our only method of discipleship. If discipleship at its core is being bound to God's will, isn't service then discipleship? Isn't wrestling with the questions of God in conversation discipleship? Isn't sacrificing our needs for the sake of someone far from God discipleship? The plea is that we no longer allow our groups to be held hostage by the church's formal weekly Bible study when the door is swinging wide with ways to explore God.

No Excuses

Unfortunately, the last issue of discipleship in our small groups hits a little harder. It doesn't come with a history or an excuse, just a reality. The reality is that discipleship, even the flawed definition, simply isn't happening in groups. Our current methods aren't creating followers of Jesus; they are creating yet another nice Christian subculture that operates within itself.

To further expound upon this point, I was going to revisit my small groups experience in Nashville. However, as I was reading back through the story, something interesting stuck out to me: About three-quarters of the entire retelling was about my wife and I actually getting into the small group. It didn't take long to summarize what it was like once we were actually there. What is worse, it took less than a page to explain what discipleship and prayer looked like.

Why is that?

The sad reality is there wasn't much to say on the subject. The total collective hours of study in that group had no lasting impact on my life. Our leaders did their best, but the church gave them no training, no mission, and no vision. The church simply handed the leaders a book and told them that if they could read it they could lead it.

Is this what we are so afraid to sacrifice? So nervous to remove from its high place?

This same thing is happening on a weekly basis all over the country. Leaders are reading a canned lesson to an unengaged crowd. Then we pray, give our hugs, say goodbye, and do it all over again the next week. Call it laziness or insanity, but the next week we flip open lesson two and hope for different results.

Let's say we find a great study (they are out there) and everyone loves it. We're still not using it to turn out disciples. The message stays in the living room where we all smile and nod, claiming that it speaks right to our life. We ingest the message, chewing and chewing until we become these fattened cows that can't move. A nice, full Christian subculture that sits inside a living room talking about how to change the world.

We have to break down and admit that our current method simply isn't getting the job done. Bible study, group lesson, or whatever you want to call it will always have some place in groups. The irony is that we give it so much time and so much power and yet so little care. We need to decide if it is important or not.

If it's important, then let's make it important. Let's relentlessly train our leaders to strengthen our study time and figure out how to make diving into the Word of God real and life changing. Let's equip our leaders with the resources to be confident in their leadership.

> This is a constant source of frustration and tension for me. I want every person in our church to lead a group and stake their claim in the priesthood of all believers. However, I know that most of them shouldn't. Even the vast majority of people who should lead need further training and support if they are going to effectively pastor a group of people into a more meaningful experience of God's Word.

If it's not important, let's chuck it. It seems like we have come to be okay with knowing that what we do is mediocre—and that is not acceptable for people serving a perfect God.

Discipleship is not designed to be a time-filler; it is designed to be a life-changer. Let's hold it to that standard. No more "if you can read it, you can lead it." If the church is not committed to the process, why would anyone else be? At the same time, let's be honest about what we're giving up and explore discipleship in every way possible.

On Mission: For Group Discussion

- What are we saying to someone who doesn't yet know Christ when they walk into a group and sit through an unengaging and irrelevant study?

- The Great Commission and the Gospel are inseparable. You make disciples by sharing the good news of Christ. The method of sharing shows itself in various forms. What methods are being used in our small groups to connect people to Christ?

- The pushback will be that small groups are for discipleship of the saved. The question is, what draws you closer to God—participating in a topical study or finding new ways to creatively communicate the Gospel, uncovering tough questions, and serving alongside someone far from God?

- What is the danger of elevating study as the central focus of all we do in groups?

- What are we denying a non-Christian by subconsciously suggesting that discipleship and study are one in the same?

Discipleship Explained

There are several Greek words our English Bible translations use for the word "disciple." The two most frequently used are ακολουθεω (to follow) and μαθητης (to bind or bound one). While ακολουθεω is pretty straightforward—Jesus said, "Follow me," and they followed him—μαθητης is a much more interesting theological term.

μαθητης was an acquisition of knowledge that sank in so deep that it literally changed one's nature. This was done by binding oneself completely to a master teacher in order to observe not only his teachings but every facet of his life.

Where it gets fascinating is in Deuteronomy, where we find that God's people are to bind themselves to the Torah instead of a person. The Torah was the witness to God's saving relationship with his people and his plan for blessing the nations. It was his people, bound to his Word, living out his will through the law that would ultimately make his name known.

Where it becomes utterly mind-blowing is in the person of Jesus Christ. God's Word became man and lived among his people. God Incarnate made God's will appear in flesh and bones and blood. In first century Palestine, people were able to quite literally bind themselves to the whole story of God's saving relationship with his people through a real relationship with a person—Jesus.

Now because of the resurrected Christ, we are able to continue to enjoy that same relationship with Jesus, whose spirit dwells in us, and we are therefore completely bound too.

This is what it means to be a disciple: To be bound completely to God's will through a tangible relationship with God's Word as God's Spirit lives in and through us—it's a fundamental redirection of our existence.

I'm one of the last people in the cosmos who would downplay the role of Bible study or loving God with all your mind, but any discussion of a disciple-making process must begin and end with an outward orientation. Why? Because making a disciple is merely helping someone else encounter God's will. Which, thankfully, is his saving relationship with his people.

That is grace.

Jesus said to Peter, "Come, follow me, and I will show you how to fish for people!" (Matthew 4:19). It's been said so beautifully that "grace becomes an event in such a calling."[1] All the images of disciples are active—learning, following, binding, fishing—because action precludes living.

The grace event in our lives is what makes a disciple. Jesus does the binding. Our role is doing the difficult work of following Jesus in his work of compassion, because in the end, that means an unconditional sacrifice of our whole lives.

Chapter 5

CULTURAL COW #3: ACCOUNTABILITY

BY ZACH

Playing the Politician

Throughout college, I flip-flopped like a politician when it came to what I was going to do with my life. I walked onto campus knowing that I wanted to be a youth pastor. That changed when I realized that most junior high students have a distinct smell that my nose does not appreciate. From there, I decided I was going to be a missionary. After three months in Africa, I rethought my plan. Then to really drive my parents crazy, I pulled a complete 180 and transferred schools, set on being a sports agent. That was short lived, and I transferred back to my first college because I thought I had it right the first time: youth pastor. I must have driven my parents utterly mad. One of my vocational hiccups along the way was to become a small groups minister.

Small groups were a buzzing concept around the church world, and more and more churches were starting to hire full-time ministers for this role. Honestly, I didn't really know much about small groups, but I had been in plenty of group Bible studies and figured they were just a trendy word for the same thing. More than anything I thought, "Hey, if I could work at a church and never have to preach or entertain kids and still get paid, sign me up!"

I remember sitting in a class called *Dynamics of Small Groups*, and the topic of the day was accountability. Our professor told us that accountability was a central piece of small groups and we needed to get comfortable with the idea. He asked us to break into groups of 6 to 8 and role-play, asking accountability questions in a small-group format. We had a list of questions in our books, and we each took a turn pretending to lead a small group through an accountability exercise.

I read through the questions. They were questions like:

- Have you compromised your integrity in any way?

- Has your thought life been pure?

- Are you satisfied with the time you spent with the Lord this week?

- Did you control your tongue?

- What one sin plagued your walk with God this week?

- How have you demonstrated a servant's heart?

- Did you treat your peers and co-workers as people loved by God?

That was the last small groups class I ever took.

> This story cracks me up every time I hear it. Are you kidding me?! Can you imagine that! Who would ever invite anyone into that setting? Perfect example for the adage that university professors should be forced to enter into the workforce for a year of service every five years or so.

This class came at the worst time in my spiritual journey. I was just emerging out of high school—a place where I was constantly trying to figure out how to juggle the need to be popular, the "rules" of being a Christian, and deep spiritual questions that made me feel like a fraud. I didn't know how to be a Christian and deal with the doubts and questions in my heart. In my experience, church was not the place to ask such questions. I was searching for a place or relationship in my life where I could open up a real dialogue about my faith issues. I was looking for authenticity somewhere within the church, and that list of questions sucked the wind right out of me.

My first thought was, "Who talks like this?" The questions seemed like they were almost written in another language. I also remember feeling like it summed up my worst fears about church—that it was irrelevant, uncommunicative, and that I was destined to struggle through faith alone.

Authenticity and accountability go hand in hand. If our groups and churches are struggling with authenticity, then accountability is doomed. I didn't know much as a young college kid, but I was smart enough to know when a list of questions felt canned, non-conversational, and a far cry from authentic.

The Real Accountability Questions

The claims my professor made back in the early 2000s are the same claims we make today. We claim that accountability is a necessary and integral part of small groups. We claim that it is an intentional piece of what we do, alive and powerful. In the past, I made that same claim when I pitched small groups to my students and elders. I would never make such a claim today. It's time to talk openly and honestly about the relationship between accountability and groups. When discussing this claim, we need to wrestle with a few questions.

What are we talking about when we make the claim that our groups offer accountability?

The unfortunate truth is that we are not saying much at all on the subject, leaving it wide open for interpretation. Accountability is one of those Christianese words that stands on its own island. We use it and hope that everyone understands what it means. When in reality, the average person who fills our church worship centers and auditoriums on Sunday morning does not have a clear understanding of the concept of Christian accountability.

Our Top 5 Words Only Christians Use		
1. Sanctification	3. Fellowship	5. Edification
2. Traveling Mercies	4. Backsliding	

What happens when a person is forced to interpret and internalize a concept that remains unclear? Perception becomes reality. For many people, the perception of accountability in small groups is the picture of people sitting in a circle, sharing a box of tissues, and being forced to reveal the deepest failures of their life. Whether or not this is an accurate picture of accountability in small groups matters little; the perception is what matters, and the perception is enough to scare people away.

People also get a perception-building dose of the idea of accountability from movies. There are countless films out there that portray an angry boss or some person of authority standing in a boardroom, slamming his or her fist on the table, and yelling, "Someone's going to be held accountable for this!" Again, not building a real positive perception of accountability.

People just need one reason *not* to do something. For some, the fear of the word *accountability* is enough to keep them out of groups. Understandable. Nowhere else in life is it natural to reveal yourself publically to people who you don't share a deep connection with. If we can replace this false perception of accountability with a clear picture of what accountability should look like in our groups, we can take away one more obstacle for those who are anxious about joining a group.

Is accountability really happening in our groups?

Again, without a clear understanding of accountability, perception wins out. Luckily, the perception of accountability gets shattered quickly by the second little claim about accountability in small groups—we don't do it.

This should not be that surprising. How can we practice accountability when we are not even sure to what we're supposed to be holding people accountable? This is one of the first bubbles to burst for people who are nervous about joining a group for the first time. They breathe a sigh of relief and say things like, "Man, I thought we were just going to sit around and share our feelings or that I was going to have to confess all my sins in front of everyone."

In a sense, statements like this are sad, because it just pushes people away from a very biblical concept. Relational accountability is something we all need in our life, but the lack of understanding of how it fits into the small group setting causes us to abandon the concept completely.

On the other hand, we breathe a sigh of relief when we realize that people aren't really holding us to the claims we make about accountability. If leadership isn't addressing the concept, then we don't have to be intentional about it. We can just say it's an important piece of small groups and hope it happens naturally.

Tullian Tchividjian wrote a great article for RELEVANT magazine in February 2012 on accountability. In the article he says, "My greatest need (and yours) is to look at Christ more than we look at ourselves, because the Gospel is not my work for Jesus, but Jesus' work in me. It takes the loving act of our Christian brothers and sisters to remind us every day of the Gospel—that everything we need, and everything we look for, is already ours, 'in Christ.' When we do this, the 'good stuff' rises to the top."[1]

But there is a bigger reason we feel so relieved that we don't have to implement intentional accountability. The answer lies within the next question.

Are small groups the proper place for accountability?

This leads us to the claim that we all feel in our gut but don't want to admit. It's the main reason we're not intentional about accountability in our groups. The truth is that the current perception of accountability doesn't belong in a small group setting.

In no way am I discrediting the idea or need of relational accountability. I firmly believe you need at least one or two people in your life to fill that role, but I don't believe this belongs in a public small group setting. Having a small group fill that role is actually a huge deterrent to authenticity. If groups that have met together once a week for 6 months are asking these deep and personal questions, especially in the unnatural form that I experienced in my class, then we are breeding an inauthentic group. We are essentially forcing someone to hide, embellish, or lie about their spiritual journey, because it's too soon to honestly expose themselves in front of a large group. Who would? It is an unrealistic expectation for our group members. It is hard enough to fully reveal yourself to those closest to you. To reveal yourself out loud in a group setting is not a step we should ask people to take.

Pick a Verse, Any Verse

So where did this idea of accountability in groups come from? There are times when church leaders take liberty with context and grab verses that authenticate our cause or program. It is not because they are trying to be misleading. It's simply that leaders are excited about a program and want it to be anchored in Scripture. The champion verse of accountability is James 5:16: "Confess your sins to each other and pray for each other so that you may be healed. The earnest prayer of a righteous person has great power and produces wonderful results."

This is an obvious call for accountability. James says it is important to talk about your struggles and pray for each other so that you have someone battling through the struggle and praying alongside you. However, the verse does not say, "Confess your sins to each other every Thursday night from 6:00-7:30 p.m. during small group time so that you may be healed."

So my question is, why do we keep championing this version of accountability? We know it is not a biblical mandate. We know it is not natural. We know it can be a deterrent to authenticity and mission. Furthermore, we know it is not genuinely happening. All the while we are still claiming it as an important part of what we do in groups.

The Cost

There is a cost to the church's lack of clarity and intentionality concerning the concept of accountability. The currently held (and sometimes implemented) expression has created a fear of the word *accountability*. You simply say the word and people get nervous. In all honesty, I cringe a little when people bring it up. Without knowing what their perception of accountability is, it's impossible to know what they are suggesting for our groups. The result is that we close the door on any form of accountability in groups.

While the perception says otherwise, not all forms of accountability are invasive and uncomfortable. After all, we can hold each other accountable to small steps of faith, whether it be service, reading a chapter of Scripture, or prayer. Austin will address the practical side of accountability in groups in Chapter 11, "Paradigm Shift #1: The Bible Says."

For now, let's agree to put this claim to rest. Let's finally admit out loud that a small group is not the place for the currently held expression of accountability. By releasing ourselves from the idea that the main place accountability should happen is in groups, we can actually start talking about it again. We can explore what accountability could really look like and focus on the most natural, relational way to encourage accountability. If the ongoing experiment of Christian community has taught us anything, it is that authentic accountability does not flow out of group discussion; it flows out of meaningful relationships.

On Mission: For Group Discussion

If your group has a deep bond of accountability, I understand the fear of losing it. Our desire is not that you would sacrifice accountability. If the bond truly runs deep in your group, then it shouldn't be hard to maintain that accountability outside of group time. However, we need to filter accountability through our mission. In everything we do, we have to remember that our mission is to help those far from God experience Jesus.

If a non-Christian walked into one of our groups and witnessed what we call accountability, their takeaways would likely be…

- **We don't take it seriously, so it must not hold any real value.** The fact that we claim small groups offer accountability without really doing it diminishes the true power of accountability. True relational accountability can fuel you. Having someone in your life to help you steer through the highs and lows of faith can free you and challenge you. While I fully believe this, not many would claim the same from their experience in groups. Instead of seeing the power of relational accountability, a witness would likely see something closer to a meaningless ritual. Something that must be required for church members but offers no real value.

- **Either the people are not authentic, or the group is not accepting.** Anyone could witness that the members of small groups still get uncomfortable and guarded when questions go too deep. Like I discussed earlier, when we try to get too personal too quickly, it forces members to either shut down, blow the question off with a one-word answer, or pander to appease the group. Any of these responses would cause a non-Christian to doubt the real impact that both the group and God have on our lives.

- **Count me out!** People who have not been around small groups don't get it. Why would anyone want to openly share that stuff with people they barely know? A non-Christian or visitor is likely sitting around thinking, "Don't call on me; don't call on me." Even if they are not called on to share, they will likely walk out thinking they escaped a very uncomfortable situation and will not return.

- **I would be a total outsider in this group.** This is especially true for those groups that do have very real accountability. If someone walked into a group where everyone was sharing on a deep personal level, the obvious thought would be, "I would not fit in this group." It likely took a group years to get to that level, and truthfully, a new member would never get there.

Which of these insights would a non-Christian receive from your small group?

Chapter 6

CULTURAL COW #4: NATURAL AND INVITING

BY ZACH

Pretty Pictures

Small group resources love to paint a picture of happy people in living rooms. Everyone is smiling, the rooms are always painted in soft earth tones, and the food looks like it was photographed by the same guy who shoots the pictures of french fries for McDonalds' menu board. I tell you what, that guy has some kind of gift. In small group photos, people are laughing like they are all best buddies and ignoring all the societal norms of personal space. Take a look at the photo on the left page for a perfect example of what I'm talking about. What are photos like this saying? They are saying, "Our small group is inviting and natural."

The interesting thing about this claim is that it is both entirely true and at the same time completely false. The truth of this claim is predicated by your circumstance. In my life I have both agreed with and scoffed at the claim that our groups are inviting and natural.

What changed?

The basic tenants of groups didn't change. There were always couches, food, people, lessons, and icebreakers. It was simply the circumstance surrounding my involvement in those groups that changed. As a result, what was true at one time became entirely false at a later time.

While it may seem like I am talking in nonsensical circles, the truth is pretty simple. If you are reading this book, you fall into one of three camps. Your agreement or disagreement with small groups' claims of being inviting and natural will depend on which camp you reside in.

Camp #1—You have been a member of the same church for years. You know everyone, and everyone knows you.

Camp #2—You are a Christian, but you are currently trying to get involved in a new church or a new group.

Camp #3—You are an explorer, and someone invited you to church or a small group. You know a couple of people there.

Camp #1

If you're in this camp, then you probably don't know what all the fuss is about. You know everyone at church, and everyone at church knows you. You've sat in the same seat or pew for years, and you go to lunch with the minister every Tuesday. For you, church is easy. Your small group probably meets at a good friend's house and is mostly made up of people you have known for years. If you are in Camp 1, the claim that small groups are natural and inviting is absolutely true. I've been in Camp 1. It's wonderful. When I was in Camp 1, I wore sweatpants to group and didn't worry about combing my hair. Camp 1 is comfy and nice.

Camp #2

The church starts playing with the words *inviting* and *natural* very liberally when dealing with those in Camp 2. For those new to a church, nothing screams unnatural more than a church-wide group sign-up. And just because our groups are held at a place that has couches and easy chairs doesn't automatically mean it is inviting. It's much easier to hide in the comfort of the crowd in a worship center. I've been in Camp 2. I've knocked on a stranger's door, sat in a circle, and been bombarded with questions from strangers. That's not natural—that's stressful!

The good news for the church is that most people in Camp 2 will probably put up with the awkwardness. The need for some form of community, however flawed, will outweigh the attempt to avoid discomfort. If that isn't enough, some good old church guilt will bridge the gap and keep them going week in and week out.

Obviously the church does not want either of those reasons to be the deciding factor for group involvement. Most people in church leadership reside in Camp 1. Our leaders need to be very aware that Camp 2 does exist, that they are different from those in Camp 1, and that its members want to be involved. For newcomers to a church or community, it is a stressful and scary process to step forward into deeper involvement.

We should always be wrestling with the question, "How can we make groups a more natural process for people in Camp 2?"

Camp #3

So if we're struggling to meet the needs of Camp 2, do you think our groups are inviting and natural for Camp 3? For those in Camp 3, our claims are an outright lie. If we are honest, there is nothing natural or inviting about a stranger walking into another stranger's house, making small talk, eating their snacks, and talking in a circle. Do you know what that is? It is every faculty party I've ever had to go to with my wife.

My wife, Jaime, went to 9 straight years of college, which either makes her brilliant or crazy! Every year of her Ph.D. program, there was a faculty/student Christmas party. I would be forced to go out and buy a Christmas sweater that I would only wear once, cram a collared shirt underneath it, and put on khakis (this is a real stretch for me). Then we'd walk up and ring the doorbell of some professor I didn't know.

If you have ever been in this situation, you know these experiences drag drudgingly along. First off, I might as well have worn a T-shirt and shorts, because no matter what the temperature was outside, it was 85 degrees in the house and I was wearing three layers. Nothing makes an awkward situation more awkward than adding sweat to the occasion.

I would usually hang around the food table. If nothing else, they always had a great spread that kept me looking busy. I'd be munching on a cheese ball or bacon-wrapped something, and people would come up and chat about sports or the weather or how great it was that I was a minister and how they grew up in this church or that church. Before long, we'd run out of small talk and just be staring at one another smiling. When the awkwardness reached its apex, one of us would fake a phone call, ask where the bathroom was, or say "I'm gonna go get my hands on one of those crab cakes" and walk off. It was generally 70 percent brutal, 20 percent tolerable, and 10 percent fun. I'd always walk away saying, "That was okay, considering."

If you were in the program like Jaime and her classmates, you'd fit right in. If you were arm candy (I use that term very loosely) like myself and a few other spouses, it was a completely different experience.

Aren't we offering the same circumstances in our small groups? If you are a part of the program (a Christian), chances are you'll fit right in. However, if someone who is not a member of the "God club" walks in, they are probably going to be sweating, chatting around the food table, and walking away saying, "That was brutal." At least Jaime's Christmas parties provided social lubricants to ease the pain. I haven't met a ton of small groups that offer alcohol on a weekly basis (nor am I suggesting it).

Let's flip the situation around on believers. What is the most inviting place in the history of TV land? Here's a hint: The theme song is "Where Everybody Knows Your Name." That's right, *Cheers!* From 1982 to 1993 and into rerun history, *Cheers* was the most inviting place on TV. After all, everybody knows your name, they're "always glad you came," and they'll listen to your problems and try to help you through it. If they can't, they'll buy you a beer and drink with you until you drown those problems. Sounds a little bit like a small group to me (other than the binge drinking). Sam, Woody, Norm, and Cliff were the nicest guys around. How could anyone be nervous or apprehensive about walking in and chatting it up with them? Yet, I know many Christians who would feel wildly out of place there. To people in the club (the *Cheers* crowd), it's a no-brainer; but to someone not accustomed to that environment, it becomes uncomfortable, stressful, and probably out of the question.

And of course there is another "camp"—Camp 4. These are the people who are the stated focus of our mission in the first place. Someone far from God isn't even in the larger discussion in this context of the typical small group model. The last descriptors to come to mind if they were to step into the group time would be natural and inviting.

True and False

This is another perfect example of how groups are wildly successful but still missing the mark. We call it natural and inviting because—if you're reading this—you are probably in or around the "God club." As a Camp 1 Christian, it is not that hard to walk into a group and get assimilated, because it is a natural progression. Go to church, and join a group or team. It's what we hear weekly, so the concept is not foreign to us. Even those in Camp 2 are at least familiar with the process—no matter how agonizing it may be.

For Camp 3, the methods are completely foreign. The whole idea feels like another weird ritual or tradition the church is implementing. You may think I'm exaggerating, but if you look around the rooms at our small groups, it doesn't take long to realize that something is missing—Camp 3. The very nature of our group design is functioning with no thought for this people group. You may be saying, "Yes, it's tough for those in Camp 3, but small groups are more for people in Camps 1 and 2—for those who already know God." It's true that our groups have operated that way traditionally. But again, how can we give something so much time and attention and not filter it through our mission? We have to ask, are our claims true not only for Christians but for people who are far from God? Most of the time small groups are natural and inviting for those who know God; however, take some time and really ask yourself, your leadership team, and your church how it would feel to someone outside the club.

Vicious Cycles and Ironic Coins

There's another ironic side of the coin. It is found in our claim that our groups are so very inviting. When the truth is...*we never invite anyone!*

> This point breaks my heart...and I'm just as guilty of it as anyone. Being a small group pastor, I am constantly inviting Christians into groups, but I often go long stretches of time in which I don't invite a single "unchurched" person into my own group.

If our groups are truly inviting as they claim, shouldn't actually inviting people be a natural consequence? It's really a cyclical problem. The only way we can make groups a remotely natural process is through an invitation that comes out of a real, invested relationship. However, we ignore the invite of our so-called inviting small groups. As a result, we are forced to conduct events like group sign-ups and open houses, which in the end cause our groups to feel very uninviting and unnatural. If we want our groups to actually fulfill what we proclaim them to be, we need to form them out of our daily lives. We need to form them out of service and out of our natural relationships.

On Mission: For Group Discussion

- The mission implication is simple. More than likely, those in Camp 3 will not be going through our group sign-ups. They're not going to step foot in an open house environment like I experienced in Nashville. If we don't intentionally invite people from Camp 3, they will never step foot in our small groups. Do you agree? Why or why not?

- How can we design our group time so that those in Camp 3 can get to know and be comfortable around other members of the group? By the way, icebreakers are not the answer here!

- If we stay huddled in our living rooms waiting for people to come to us, we are going to be waiting a long time. Would another venue make more sense?

- There is another group we are ignoring entirely. Austin called it Camp 4. This group consists of people not searching for God at all, whether purposefully or simply by living unexamined. We can never make our living rooms so comfortable that they will just show up. How could a small group reach these people?

- Something is broken if we have the greatest gift in the world to give and we are not inviting others to experience it. We should be just as excited to invite people into our small group as we are to our cool, hip, trendy, contemporary Sunday morning worship services. Our groups should be acting as a "front door" into church. Why aren't they?

Chapter 7

CULTURAL COW #5: AUTHENTIC

BY ZACH

The Snorkeling Rhinoceros

I always wanted a cool nickname. I grew up watching WWF wrestling, and all those guys had awesome names like Brutus "The Barber" Beefcake, Jimmy "Superfly" Snuka, and "Macho Man" Randy Savage. I wanted to be just like them. I wanted a name that said, "This guy is more than just Zach—he is…the 'Snorkeling Rhinoceros'!" or something awesome like that. By the way, "Snorkeling Rhinoceros" is the first thing that jumped into my head, which shows just how miswired my brain truly is. Although now the name is starting to grow on me…

Most nicknames have little validity when it comes to the actual self. Brutus "The Barber" Beefcake didn't really moonlight as a licensed barber. Nor did he really walk around putting strangers in sleeper holds so he could secretly cut their hair. Nicknames are exaggerations—generally inauthentic and self-given. However, one boxer earned a nickname that itself *is* the definition of authenticity.

Top 5 Greatest Sports Nicknames of All Time

5. Dr. Dunkenstein (Darryl Dawkins)

4. The Round Mound of Rebound (Charles Barkley)

3. The Fridge (William "Refrigerator" Perry)

2. The Great One (Wayne Gretzky)

1. The Flying Tomato (Shaun White)

Evander Holyfield will likely always be remembered for "The Bite Fight," when Mike Tyson bit off a chunk of his ear. However, Holyfield earned his legendary and appropriate nickname, "The Real Deal," long before that day. "The Real Deal" Holyfield was the undisputed world champion in both cruiserweight and heavyweight, and he is the only 4-time World Heavyweight Champion. My favorite definition of *authentic*, which I came across on dictionary.com, is "having the origin supported by unquestionable evidence." That was Holyfield. Proven. Authentic. "The Real Deal."

We love to use the term *authentic* in our small group marketing. We say that groups are a place where you can come and be the real you. Jump in, let your hair down, and take off the mask. The question is, what are we even trying to get at with all this authentic talk? What does it mean for our groups to be authentic? How do you define "authentic community"? Holyfield earned his nickname of "The Real Deal." Have our small groups earned the right to be titled authentic?

Tri-Focals

So how do we know if we are truly creating authentic communities?

Authenticity is not revealed on the surface. Once under the microscope, we see that we can't simply judge or define our groups' authenticity based on one overarching concept. To be declared an authentic community, we must look at the pieces that make up the whole. In order to answer this question, we need to look at authentic community through three different lenses:

1. Authentic Relationships

2. Authentic Selves

3. Authentic Acts

As we examine these lenses of authenticity, remember how we chose to define authentic:

- Having the origin supported by unquestionable evidence

- Not false or copied; genuine

- "The Real Deal" Holyfield

Authentic Relationships—West Side Rowdies

I love where I grew up. The west side of Evansville, Indiana is a subculture in and of itself. It's a living, breathing organism that is steeped in tradition. There are not a lot of transplants on the west side, and homes don't go up for sale very often. My mom and dad went to Reitz High School, my wife and I went to Reitz High School, and if we have our choice, our children will go to Reitz High School.

One of the things I love about life on the west side is that people hang on to relationships. I count myself very lucky that I'm still friends with many of the people I went to high school with. As a matter of fact, every year I attend a Halloween party thrown by one of my good friends from Reitz. This friend ended up marrying his high school sweetheart, another good friend of mine. The same people have been coming to this party for years. My wife and I have been coming ever since it started as a crazy party full of single people up on Reitz Hill. Now the party has changed drastically. Our friends now make up families, the loud music has been turned down, all streaking has ceased, and the beer mugs have been exchanged for sippy cups. There are dozens of kids running around, and grown men now dress as Tweedledee and Tweedledum instead of zombies and werewolves. I love that!

I've been friends with most of these people for almost 20 years. They have seen me at my absolute worst, and I have been around for their highs and lows as well. These friends stayed true through all phases of life. They were present and accounted for during my "super-judgmental Christian phase," with me during my "I want no part of

God phase," and they are still relevant today in my current unclassified form. We have 20 years of history with every conversation.

Why does this matter?

It matters because for the longest time I thought I had to have that level of depth and history to call any relationship authentic. It took a long time to realize that if I'm judging every relationship by these standards, if members of our groups are judging relationships by these standards, then they will miss the mark every time. It can't be duplicated.

I was convinced we had to somehow manufacture this depth of relationship in our groups for them to be a success. Much of the blame can be put on small groups as a whole. My take was that if groups were really going to be natural and inviting, if we were really going to hold each other accountable in a deep way and "do life together," then small groups had to be made up of a group of really good friends in order to actually live out the claims.

To some degree that is true. It is a consequence of our overselling of small groups. We put great pressure on ourselves by implementing pieces that call for this level and depth of relationship. It's why it is so essential that we shed light on the claims of small groups and talk openly about the realistic potential and limitations of them.

Authentic Relationships—Can We?

It is unrealistic to think that our group members are all going to turn into best friends who share matching heart necklaces. The fact that we are Jesus-followers does not mean we will automatically click with everyone. Some people we naturally connect with; some we don't. The good news is that we don't have to share a deep connection to still have meaningful, authentic relationships. While we cannot manufacture the type of camaraderie that comes with a 20-year history, we can promote and produce authentic relationships within our groups.

So, can we? Yes.

Do we? We'll talk more about that in Chapter 8 when we discuss the seven principles of life together.

Authentic Selves—Mike 2.0

I have a friend named Mike who is in my small group. Austin and I have both known him since high school. Mike has an absolutely contagious enthusiasm for life and has been so for as long as I have known him. He is energetic, hilarious, and intelligent. You can start a conversation with Mike about physics, his kids, or what dogs would say if they could talk, and he will engage each subject equally and with the same amount of passion. He is wide open. Some nights when we are hanging on his porch or around his fire pit, our conversations get pretty deep. We talk truthfully about life as it really is in that moment. Someone once told me that in terms of friendship, "I'd rather have four quarters than a hundred pennies." Mike is one of the quarters in my life.

What's crazy is the fact that the rest of our small group does not know Mike. They know small-group Mike. Small-group Mike is the floppy disc version of Mike 2.0. He faithfully attends weekly, but in that house for that hour and a half he generally sits guarded and unengaged. I don't know small-group Mike.

> Mike is one of my very best friends. We have truly lived life together. I have watched him go from not identifying himself with Christianity or the church to what we would call an "explorer." We often sit around his fire pit and talk openly about doubts, questions, concerns, excitement, and many other issues of faith. These discussions are honest and genuine. Unfortunately, these same discussions never take place during our group time.

The Elusive Self

The problem with claiming that we are an "authentic community" is that a community is made up of a bunch of individual people. Each individual person in any given community either promotes or deters authenticity. The goal is to create a place that fosters and encourages people to move from deter-ers to promoters.

Easier said than done. Life has taught each of us to learn and adapt so we can thrive in any group. How much and what we reveal of ourselves to our work group is likely different than what we reveal to our friend group, which is likely different than what we reveal to our church group. Our desire to fit into a group creates shields that we keep up until we discover what is and is not "acceptable" in each situation.

We struggle to be our authentic selves in Christian community. Common sense would say that as Christians we should feel the most freedom to be our true, open self in Christian community around other believers. After all, they understand the reality of the struggle when faith and life collide. However, the paradox is that we are, in fact, the opposite. Generally it is around other Christians, specifically Christians we don't know well (who have not revealed what is and is not "acceptable"), that we feel the need to hide pieces of our real selves.

This was never more evident than walking on to my Christian college campus freshman year. The simple fact was that we were all just getting out of high school and still trying to define ourselves. We all spent the last four years of high school trying to figure out how to make sense of being a Christian, while juggling the need for popularity and enduring social pressures. None of us had it together.

I definitely didn't have it together. Sure, I was a Christian. I would say I was even a lover of Jesus—a broken and highly flawed lover of Jesus (I still am). I would spend my weeks at Christian college quoting Scripture, trying to spew holy philosophical truths, and acting like I was the perfect Christ-follower. Then I'd go home for the weekend and party with all my university friends. However, the truly destructive thing I did in my attempt to play the perfect Christian was bury the doubts, negative thoughts, and deep questions I held about faith. I felt that if I voiced those deep questions that were really on my heart, then all these great Christians around me would think I was a fraud or a heretic. Even more, I thought maybe I *was* a fraud.

It took a while to realize that I wasn't alone. It turns out everyone was playing the game to some degree. Some of my friends were revered as "High Christians" because their moms or dads were professors, missionaries, or leading some East Coast Christian movement. I went home with them for the weekend and saw that they were doing the same things I was. We were all struggling. In fact, it was two professors' kids who taught me how to smoke. We would drive out to the tiny local airport and smoke cloves (We were idiots!). Then, back on campus around other believers and faculty, we would put back on our perfect Christian personas.

The Battle Continues

This is not something that only immature college kids deal with. We battle every day to be our authentic selves. For me, this battle still peeks its head out when I first meet a new Christian or fellow worship minister. Until a person reveals their flaws, the temptation is to play the perfect Christian and hide the real struggle that still comes with being a Christian. The problem is that when I play the game, it in turn causes the person I'm talking with to play along with me.

It has been falsely pounded into our heads that Christians are supposed to look, act, and think a certain way. We're afraid that if we color outside those tightly defined lines, we will be called an imposter. We want "good" Christians to think that we are "good" too—that we are worthy of being in the God club. I'm not saying we should drop truth bombs on people the moment we meet them.

"Hi, I'm Zach. I'm a lover of Jesus, but at the same time I have questions and doubts that I can't really reconcile. Sometimes I like to have a cigar, and on occasion I will drink more than one beer. Also, I think cats might be the earthly form of Satan."

Okay, that might be taking it a little far. The truth is, we keep people at a distance when we feel like we need to protect our persona. It is exhausting, destructive, and causes us to forfeit a deeper relationship with both God and those around us. Abandoning the persona for our true self is freeing and offers freedom to those around us as well.

My First Small Group

I played basketball in college. My sophomore year, a guy name Joel transferred to join our team. I was drawn to him the moment he walked onto campus. We were sitting up in his dorm room eating pizza, and with no reserve, he took a bite of pepperoni and said, "What's the point of church?" He went on to say something like, "I mean seriously, we dress up, sing songs, and leave. What is the point?"

I looked around the room at the other guys in the room. These guys had been playing the "perfect Christian game" with me for the last year, and we didn't talk like that. We didn't ask those questions. But Joel just kept on. He continued asking the questions that I had struggled with for years, and for the first time my doubts received a voice. It was liberating—completely freeing! Turns out the other guys had some of the same doubts or realized that they needed to wrestle with these questions maybe for the first time.

Those guys became my first small group. We didn't call ourselves a small group. We didn't have a set time to meet. Sometimes it happened in a dorm room; sometimes it happened at Steak 'N Shake or the bus on the way to a game in Michigan. Regardless, that group made a deeply freeing impact on my life and changed me forever.

How Does This Affect Our Group

I guarantee someone is sitting in your small group with deep burning questions that need to be voiced. Unfortunately, if history is any judge, he or she will never voice them for fear of being thrown out of the God club. You can be that freedom for someone else. The only way to authentic community is for members of our groups to have the freedom to be their authentic selves.

Authentic Acts

If a community is going to be deemed authentic, then they must act authentically. This is a fairly simple and obvious concept.

Our town has an organization called ECTA. It is the Evansville Community Tennis Association. Their mission is simple: to grow tennis in the Evansville community. They build tennis centers. They host tennis clinics and tournaments. They do not host book clubs. They do not have a food pantry or soup kitchen. Everything they do is to improve tennis in Evansville. They are acting as an authentic community of tennis players promoting tennis.

Another example would be a neighborhood watch. They exist to keep their neighborhood safe. Therefore, everything they do is to ensure this mission and purpose. This mission may show itself through meetings, parties, safety seminars, and neighborhood patrol, but each points to the overarching mission of keeping the neighborhood safe. My neighborhood watch is not going to go to a neighborhood on the other side of town to patrol. That would not be authentic to their community. To be an authentic neighborhood organization, they need to act on behalf of their own neighborhood.

What about our small groups? Do they have a clearly defined mission and purpose? In addition to promoting our authentic selves and authentic relationships, to truly be authentic our groups must be authentic in how they act and in what they do.

It is at this point that the banner of authenticity begins to unravel. My fear is that our group members don't really know why they are in a group. My guess is that many would say groups are for fellowship with other believers. They may use a super-churchy word like edification or simply say hanging out and having Bible study.

Even worse, how would the outside world define our actions? How would they define our groups if they even knew we existed? They would likely define our groups as a pleasant Christian subculture. They would use words like sheltered, internally-focused, or harmless. Words like mobilized or powerful wouldn't even be on their radar.

Remember how we first defined the word *authentic* as having the origin supported by unquestionable evidence? Do the actions of our groups provide unquestionable evidence that we are a community of sold out Christ-followers?

 If we are nothing more than a group of Christians who come together to chat, study, and fellowship, then we are not acting as an authentic community. <u>Sitting week after week, month after month, year after year on comfy couches in air-conditioned living rooms talking about how to change the world is not authentic action.</u>

Actions Become Authentic

Here is where the conversation can make your brain hurt. If we meet together to fellowship just because our groups are supposed to fellowship, then that is not authentic action. If we plan and complete a service project just because our groups are supposed to do service projects, then that is not authentic action. If I go hang out on a friend's porch just because I feel like hanging out on a friend's porch, then that is not authentic Christian action.

However…

If Christ is at the center of all we do, if we are making intentional decisions based on the mission of Christ, then all of a sudden everything we do becomes authentic. Intentional fellowship becomes authentic. Service surrounding mission becomes authentic. Hanging on a porch with a group of friends becomes authentic Christian action.

If we filter our lives and make intentional decisions based on helping people far from God experience Jesus—showing God's glory and life-changing power to our cities—then all actions, big and small, become authentic.

But here's the kicker. If we are consciously and intentionally living under that mission, we will have no choice but to get out of our living rooms and into our communities.

Our groups must include authentic action!

On Mission: For Group Discussion

- Are we truly inviting others into our lives, or are we only showing them the highlights?

- When we act like we have it all together, when we act like our relationship with God is always easy, what does that do to someone trying to experience God?

- If we're not open with our big faith questions, explorers will feel like they have to bottle their doubts and struggles, too. How do we change that?

- If there are no feet or actions put to what we do, explorers will think we are nothing more than a nice Christian subculture—quick to talk but slow to move. What makes Christian service authentic?

- What do your relationships outside church look like compared to those inside the church?

- Do our groups look like anything else in our lives?

Chapter 8

CULTURAL COW #6: LIFE TOGETHER

BY ZACH

What a Mess

Life is messy. As much as we would all love for our lives to fit in a nice box with a bright bow, we learn to live with an acceptable amount of chaos. What's funny is the relative nature of our chaos.

I wake up; hustle to try to cross something off my task list; hear my 18-month-old son, Beau, wake up; change his diaper; oops, he got poop on the floor so I clean that up; feed him; try to feed myself; throw clothes on him; put myself in any relatively clean clothes within a 10-foot radius; go to work; come home; have dinner, playtime, and bath time; put Beau down for bed; crash. This is my beautiful chaos.

For my 15-year-old nephew, the chaos is different but just as meaningful and real. He wakes up; sleepwalks through the getting-ready process; goes to school; fights for social hierarchy; studies for a history test; gets bombarded with questions from his mom; crams in video games, texting, and Facebook; crashes; then does it all again the next day.

Regardless of the actual reality of our situation, we both have to manage the chaos and make the most of our limited time in any given day. To top it off, we are by design social beings. Somehow in this chaos we have to make room for other people. What's more, we want and need to make room for other people.

Master Marketing

Whoever came up with the descriptor "life together" for small groups is a master marketer. It sounds so calm, so clean and tidy, almost harmonious. Who wouldn't be drawn to the thought that we can schedule meaningful relationships into this chaos? It makes us feel like we actually have control in our lives. It makes relationships just one more thing on the task list we can check off. Another cultural cow is surfacing and it begs the question, is life together truly an accurate picture of our small groups?

Grand Illusion

For many of us the illusion is there. As much as I like to believe that I do, the reality is that I do not entertain a large social life outside of babies, family, work, and errands. Most nights after putting my son to bed, I'm catching up with my wife for about an hour and then crashing. So the fact that I am seeing my small group Thursday night and then again for a few minutes at church Sunday morning feeds the illusion that those moments equal "life together." I see these people more than anyone else, so we must be doing life together.

Blame it on exhaustion, selfishness, or whatever you want to call it, but the reality is that it is not that easy to share life. We are all limited by real time constraints and real issues. To let someone else in is to invite their chaos into our already chaotic lives.

Perhaps that's why we meet together for an hour and a half a week and tag it as "life together." It makes us feel like we have deep relationships without having to share the burden that comes with deep relationships.

However, just because we long for it to be true doesn't make it true. It's time we stop settling for anything less than what we claim.

Principles of Life Together

So in the midst of the chaos, what does it mean to do life together?

Painting a picture of life together does not fit in a neat, concise paragraph; much like our life, it splatters paint all over the page. Our lives are complex, and as a natural consequence, the concept of life together is complex. To know if our groups really live life together, we need to filter our experience through some basic principles of life in relationship. We have identified seven principles of life together:

Principle #1: Life together exists in real life. We are great at being faithful to our weekly meetings. However, those meetings exist as one tiny piece of our total life. At an hour and a half, our group time together makes up 0.9 percent of our week. Obviously, that is less than 1 percent of our time. Do we really feel comfortable claiming that less than 1 percent of our time equals life together? On any percentage tracking scale, that is beyond failing.

Some might even claim that groups operate outside of real life. The hour and a half we spend in groups does not always look like the remaining 166.5 hours in our week. In groups we are collected, quieted, and coddled. It's great to have a weekly break from the chaos. We need it. But that is exactly what our groups are—a *break* from the chaos. Are we relating and involved with one another in real life outside of groups in the midst of the chaos? If we have to wait another 166.5 hours until the next time we check in, we are not living life together.

Principle #2: Life together is celebratory. Our lives are filled with high highs and low lows. Do we share them together? People outside the church know how to celebrate. They don't have a weekly scheduled meeting with one another, so celebration has to be a natural part of life. If Dusty gets promoted on a Tuesday, we're going out celebrating Tuesday night. This type of celebration is indicative of people living life together.

We can be pretty lame in the church. We have so much to celebrate but we're terrible at it. If someone in our group has a big life event worth celebrating, what do we usually do? Generally, we give it a quick minute at the beginning of group. It would probably be something like, "Hey everyone, big news. Jennifer is engaged!" Next, everyone gives a nice round of applause, high fives, and some "about times." Finally, we put the cherry on top and get crazy, "Cindy, why don't you bring some cookies next week to group and we'll celebrate."

This example proves one of two things. 1. We are either terrible at celebrating, or 2. We are not really invested in each other's lives enough to care.

People truly living life together care about each other's highs and lows, and they make it known. Can we claim that in our groups?

Principle #3: Life together has meat. There is only so long you can go on talking about the weather. It is sad that so many relationships, even relationships that have spanned decades, don't get below the surface. In these relationships, sports, weather, Facebook, and general life activity is about as far as it gets.

I don't need another relationship like that. I want something with some meat. I crave relationships that challenge and encourage me. The good news is, our groups are talking about things that matter. The bad news is, most of the time it only comes out of a formal forced time. If we are truly living life together, then the "meat of life" will extend beyond our small group time and into our natural conversations. To get there we have to buy into the next principle.

Principle #4: Life together is intentional. I'm not a good long distance friend. I really hate that about myself, but it is true. In the last 10 years, I have lived in Lincoln, Illinois, Knoxville, Tennessee, Maryville, Tennessee, Springfield, Illinois, Nashville, Tennessee, and I currently reside in Indiana. I have friends who I truly care about in each of those cities, but I am absolutely terrible at keeping up with them. I'm simply not intentional about it. The men who stood beside me at my wedding are scattered throughout Illinois, Louisiana, Kansas, Ohio, Florida, and Connecticut. Some I email once or twice a month if I'm lucky. Some I haven't spoken to in a few years. There was a time when I could completely affirm that we shared life together. I can't claim that anymore.

The members of our groups will never magically reach the relational level of doing life together by sitting in a circle together once a week. We may reach a comfort level. We may possibly even develop an actual friendship; however, the claims of life together run much deeper. <u>To reach that level we must intentionally invest in each other's lives.</u>

Principle #5: Life together takes commitment. The people in our groups are walking into a tough situation. Most of the time our members will not have a shared history. Many of the relationships forged will be brand-new relationships, and it simply takes time to learn what people are all about. We each run through a series of misinterpretations when members are shy, quiet, sarcastic, attention-driven, etc. before we have a handle on each other's personalities. It's not going to be comfortable at first. If we are ever going to reach the goal of authentic life together, each member of our group will need to make a commitment to nurture the relationships within the group.

I can't help but think of my experience in Nashville. If I'm honest, I did not make a commitment to the people in my group. In my immaturity, I threw an internal pity party over the fact that the members were not the people I expected. Looking back, it may have cost me meaningful relationships. Life together is a long-term investment.

Principle #6: Life together is personal. This principle is pretty simple. Contrary to what *How I Met Your Mother*, *Big Bang Theory*, and most TV shows imply, you cannot do life together with a group. Life is shared with individual people. Collectively those people may operate as a group, but the depth is only fueled by the individual relationships within the group.

Group dynamics make things simpler and give you the illusion of a relationship with each person. Think about the people in your group. What if over the next 10 days you had to have dinner with each person in that group individually? How are you feeling right now?

The point is that we need to be intentional about developing relationships with one another—not with a group.

Principle #7: Life together shares mission. This is the cornerstone principle of life together. It is not enough that our groups' mission be to simply meet with each other once a week and talk. If that is all we strive for, we will never be anything more than a mediocre Christian subculture.

If you told me that the next 10 years of my life in a group would be spent fellowshipping and talking about how to live out faith, I'd be gone in a second. I need more than that. If you told me that over the next 10 years our group is going to be on mission to do _____ for the kingdom of God and our city, I'm all in…every time.

Meaningful mission binds people together. It gives purpose. Even more, it leads us to a deeper level of relationship and moves us one step closer to true "life together." Nothing will bring your group closer together faster than collectively casting a vision and joining together in a shared mission.

On Mission: For Group Discussion

- If someone far from God saw the holes in our relationships and heard us calling it "life together," it would simply be one more nail in the coffin of authenticity. Do you agree?

- At the same time, if someone far from God caught hold of our groups' vision and mission and saw us *living out our faith together* in a very real way, it would be contagious. How can that be achieved?

- On a practical note, service is an easy entry point for someone far from God. Generally they would be on neutral ground, and people are more driven to make a difference in their communities now than they have been in a long time. Do you agree? Why or why not?

- What does life together really look like in today's ultra-busy culture?

- Is it possible to be more fluid with our group time? How can we make those connection points happen?

Chapter 9

CULTURAL COW #7: BIBLICAL

BY AUSTIN

Herme-whatics?

One of the biggest cultural cows of small groups, and maybe the issue that will cause the biggest pushback, is that the current model for small groups is not biblical. More precisely, small groups are not biblically mandated nor are they clearly defined in Scripture. That's not to say they are unbiblical, just that the typical American church small group of 8 to 12 Christians sitting in a living room circled up for discussion, preceded by a snack of some sort and concluded with prayer, is certainly not the "biblical model" for small group ministry.

Pretty much every theological foundation provided for small groups uses Acts 2:42-47 as the primary call for churches to be engaged and active in small groups. So I want to address this Scripture passage right away.

Before doing so, however, we have to make a quick detour into one of the classic debates concerning the interpretation of Scripture: prescriptive versus descriptive. I'll attempt to remain brief.

A Battle of the "Scriptives"

Since time eternal, Christians have debated exactly what to do with God's Word, as it was clearly initially written to some other people in some other time. The question they have tried to answer is, "What does this mean for us today, and how does it affect our actions in connection to our relationship with God?" To simplify an extremely interesting and millennia-long debate, there are basically three options for how to understand Scripture:

1. **Prescriptive:** What you find in God's Word should be prescribed to God's people for all time. An example would be: Since Jesus washed the disciples' feet, we as followers of Jesus Christ should wash each other's feet as an act of worship.

2. **Descriptive:** What you find in God's Word is a description of God's relationship with his people at a certain time and point in history and should be used to glean principles to apply to our lives today.

3. **Some combination of the two:** Obviously, this involves a wide spectrum.

> I think it is hilarious that Austin claimed he would be brief and then his very next sentence kicks off with "since time eternal."

The Great Debate

All three of these options have their problems, which is why the debate has raged on:

- Prescriptive interpretation would be nice, but then you run into denominations of snake handlers (Mark 16:17-18) and have to answer questions about why women don't speak in your church (1 Corinthians 14:34-35). You either have to accept those passages literally, ignore them, or come up with a slick way around them. None are good options.

- Descriptive interpretation of the Bible sounds nice and much more contemporary, but it can get pretty subjective pretty fast. I've heard of people partaking of Oreos and milk in the Lord's Supper and getting baptized in whipped cream.

- The third option has to be the answer, right? But who sits in judgment over which passage is prescriptive and which is descriptive? Do you elect a board? Only congregate with people who share your opinions?

Turning to Acts 2:42-47, every hippie Christian's and small group pastor's favorite verse says, "All the believers devoted themselves to the apostles' teaching, and to fellowship, and to sharing in meals (including the Lord's Supper), and to prayer" (Acts 2:42).

And in verse 46 we see that all the believers "met in homes for the Lord's Supper, and shared their meals with great joy and generosity."

Acts 2:42-47

42 All the believers devoted themselves to the apostles' teaching, and to fellowship, and to sharing in meals (including the Lord's Supper), and to prayer.

43 A deep sense of awe came over them all, and the apostles performed many miraculous signs and wonders. 44 And all the believers met together in one place and shared everything they had. 45 They sold their property and possessions and shared the money with those in need. 46 They worshiped together at the Temple each day, met in homes for the Lord's Supper, and shared their meals with great joy and generosity— 47 all the while praising God and enjoying the goodwill of all the people. And each day the Lord added to their fellowship those who were being saved.

This peek into the first century church came right after the day of Pentecost. On that day, God established his church by sending the Holy Spirit to empower the disciples to spread the good news with authority. Peter preached the first explicitly Gospel-centered sermon, and 3,000 people came to know Jesus Christ.

The model seems to be clear: large attractional services, with smaller, more intimate breakouts. Within the breakouts, or small groups, we should include the activities of studying the Bible (apostles' teachings), fellowship, prayer, and sharing a meal. Add in the information from verse 46 and we have these groups meet in homes, and the whole package is wrapped with a neat little bow. We have the "perfect" biblical small group model.

Let's unravel that bow a little bit...

Unraveling the Bow

First off, when you read the whole section together, you find that it is written in narrative form. Narrative is functionally descriptive. This passage in Acts is clearly retelling a story about people who lived in a specific point in time. When you read verses 43-44, you see some things happening that are not likely to happen again: "A deep sense of awe came over them all, and the apostles performed many miraculous signs and wonders. And all the believers met together in one place and shared everything they had."

To prescribe actions for our small groups today based on these verses becomes problematic. For instance, the magnitude, nature, and scale of the apostles' "signs and wonders" would be hard to duplicate in our routine group settings. Also, all the believers could in fact be together then, because these were all the believers in the world at the time: 3,012. It would be nearly impossible to get all 2.8 billion or so Christians together today and even more nearly impossible for them to have all things in common.

If you prescribe part of a passage, shouldn't you prescribe the rest of it? Because I have never read a small groups book or heard a teaching that prescribes verses 44-45: "And all the believers met together in one place and shared everything they had. They sold their property and possessions and shared the money with those in need."

We have so precious few glimpses of the first century church and how it operated that we tend to heighten the importance of those few times we do get a seemingly straightforward look. So much so that we idealize what we find there and say, "We want to be an Acts 2:42 church."

But how can we be an Acts 2:42 and not an Acts 2:44-45 church? Especially considering that a few chapters later (Acts 4:32-35), it isn't verses 42 and 46 that are reinforced but rather verses 43-45:

> *All the believers were united in heart and mind. And they felt that what they owned was not their own, so they shared everything they had. The apostles testified powerfully to the resurrection of the Lord Jesus, and God's great blessing was upon them all. There were no needy people among them, because those who owned land or houses would sell them and bring the money to the apostles to give to those in need* (Acts 4:32-35).

Why do we not teach that a natural part of our discipleship process, as lived out in our small groups, is to sell our possessions and lay them at the feet of our small group leaders to distribute to those in need? It may at least solve our small group leadership problems.

The answer we give, and I happen to believe is the correct one, is, "Well, that just doesn't fit our time. That wouldn't work in our day and age. It just doesn't make sense." That is true. It is a matter of context. Which is why we also don't adopt the following small group models:

- **Jethro-Moses model of small groups:** Take our large churches and break them into groups of 100s, 50s, and 10s, and appoint a man of upright character to lead the groups. They can live life in community, and whenever disputes arise, the appointed leader will exercise judgment over the disputes and settle them.

- **David's Mighty Men model of small groups:** Take our larger churches and break them into smaller groups of roaming war parties. Led by a charismatic leader, they wage war against the surrounding godless cultures.

- **Jesus' model of small groups:** Gather followers of Christ into groups of 70 for a period of intensive teaching and instruction. Then further break that group into pairs and send them out with no belongings, not even shoes, in order to walk through surrounding cities to prepare the way for the good news of Jesus Christ.

We don't adopt these models for small groups because they would be ridiculous. They do not fit the context in which we live. Yet all of these examples are most definitely biblical. These, and many more, are examples of God calling out a group of people to live in Christ-centered communities for the purpose of meeting a very real need that was present in the time and place they existed.

Uniquely Christian

The Acts church met in homes because there were no church buildings. When they gathered together corporately for worship, it was most likely at the Temple and in synagogues. Then they would break out into smaller groups and celebrate the Lord's Supper and focus on the apostles' teachings (the Gospel), because these are the things that were uniquely Christian and differentiated them from their Jewish kinsmen.

There are other instances in Acts, besides Acts 2:42, where we catch fleeting glimpses of the church gathered in small groups. In Acts 6, a small group of men are chosen to help with the distribution of food among the smaller communities of the church. In chapters 8 and 11, facing severe persecution, the church is scattered and driven into homes all throughout the geographical region. In chapter 20, Paul visits a house church (or small group); it is packed to overflowing, and the format is an all night lecture. I doubt anyone is rushing to sign up for that particular model these days.

Biblical Groups

This brings us to the second part of cultural cow #7: We don't really have a "biblical model" for small groups at all. That may seem odd coming from a small groups pastor, but the truth is Jesus doesn't give a cryptic parable concerning small group formation, none of the apostles address it, and Paul leaves no instruction. This is because small groups are not biblical.

Again, let me stress, *neither are they unbiblical.* But the typical small group model as we understand it is not prescribed by Scripture.

You could certainly make a strong argument that the above small group model is based on a description of a biblical narrative of the church and is representative of principles gleaned from the passage and applied appropriately to our modern day context. You will get no argument from me.

I just happen to believe that given our modern day context, we need to reexamine our expression of smaller group Christian communities with added emphasis on the purpose of why they exist in the first place.

When you only focus on Acts 2:42 and pepper in verse 46, you miss the middle chunk that calls into question if we are, can, or would even want to prescribe this passage to small groups. You also miss the closing, which happens to be the best part: "All the while praising God and enjoying the goodwill of all the people. And each day the Lord added to their fellowship those who were being saved" (Acts 2:47).

Whether it's Abraham's clan being sent out into covenantal relationship to bless the nations, the Hebrews breaking into small groups so justice can reign among God's people in order that they might bear witness to God's justice, or Jesus' disciples being sent out to make more disciples, the ultimate purpose of Christ-centered communities is for them to glorify God, make his name known, and bring others into a rescuing relationship with him.

The Christian Huddle

How can this ultimate purpose be realized in our culture if we remain huddled in our living rooms?

Our small groups *should* be Acts churches. Nowhere is the purpose of small groups more powerfully described than in the growth of the early church in Acts. In chapters such as 2, 4, 8, and 11 that describe the apostles' missionary journeys, we hear of exponential growth for the kingdom of God. The sweetest words in Acts are "And each day the Lord added to their fellowship" (Acts 2:47).

Wherever the church went, it flourished and spread because it was transforming lives as it went. The smaller Christian communities were meeting whenever, wherever, and however in order to live out their faith and share the good news. And as they did, they found favor among the people they lived alongside, and God used these relationships to multiply his kingdom.

That would be our biblical definition of a Christian small group: A group of people called out by God to impact another person or groups of people who are far from God for the name and purpose of Jesus Christ.

Now what does that group look like and do? Well, that is up for grabs...

On Mission: For Group Discussion

- How has the typical model for small groups acted as a gage for our understanding of living out biblical Christian community?

- The fact that we have no official biblical model leaves us wide open with options for implementing our mission. What are some ways besides small groups that we can implement our mission as the church?

- The vision of the early church found in Acts 2:42-47 (as well as other places) is a description of a uniquely Christian community inside its wider culture. Is there anything uniquely Christian about our small groups that are a contrast to the wider culture of today? How can we tap into this uniqueness during group time?

- How can we differentiate ourselves without also distancing ourselves?

Part Two:

PARADIGM SHIFTS

Chapter 10

'80s MUSIC AND SMALL GROUPS

BY AUSTIN

The Emergence of Michael W. Smith

I first became aware of pop culture music in the late '80s. One of my very first observations after reaching this awareness was that the music I heard on the radio sounded nothing like the music I heard at church.

The '80s was a decade of big hair bands like Guns N' Roses and Def Leppard, huge pop stars like Prince, Madonna, and Michael Jackson, the emergence of the metal genre with Metallica and AC/DC, and singer/songwriters like Phil Collins, George Michael, and Bruce Springsteen.

At church, hymns still reigned supreme. Organ and piano music had become so ingrained in church services that it was synonymous with worship.

If the difference between the two was obvious to an 8 year old, it was certainly clear to the rest of America. You had church music here, and way over there was the music of popular culture. There was a chasm dividing the experience people had at church and what they experienced throughout the rest of their week. On one side of the divide was the sacredness of hymns and organ music, and on the other side was the secular-ness of big hair rock and pop music.

Some forward-thinking Christians felt the tension of this gap and tried to fill the void between the church and American culture. The thinking, I assume, was that by filling the gap with music that was Christian and yet sounded mainstream, Christians could better connect with culture, and non-Christians could more easily connect with the Christian message. There's that and the more straightforward reason of those forward-thinking Christians wanting to play music they liked and connected with.

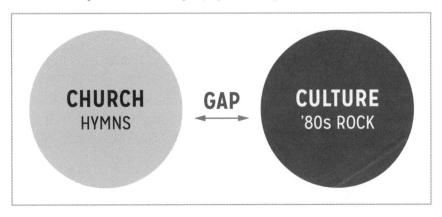

CHURCH — HYMNS ← GAP → CULTURE — '80s ROCK

The first bands/musicians I heard who sang explicitly Christian lyrics that didn't sound like "church music" were Michael W. Smith, a singer-songwriter sort of like Phil Collins and George Michael, DC Talk, who dabbled in rap and pop music, and Petra, who kind of bounced around between the hard rock and the glam rock scene.

And they were actually fairly successful. DC Talk's album *Jesus Freak* reached #16 on the Billboard 200 chart, and their best-seller *Supernatural* debuted at #4. Michael W. Smith's single "Place in This World" made it all the way to #6 on the Billboard Hot 100 chart, and his song "I Will be Here for You" was a #1 adult contemporary hit. Petra didn't have quite the level of mainstream success as the other two, but they did have this awesome album cover (scan QR code to the right) and a song called "God Gave Rock and Roll to You."

As glam rock gave way to grunge, Amy Grant and Petra gave way to bands like Newsboys, Jars of Clay, Switchfoot, and DC Talk (with their revised, updated sound). The thing all these bands had in common was that they used their artistic creativity to tap into the current music scene, while still delivering music driven by the Christian message. They were giving people an alternative to the Sunday morning experience and attempting to connect their art with the wider culture.

The Emergence of Small Groups

Small groups, as they are expressed now, really became part of the church landscape in the 1980s. A Google search will tell you the historical and biblical model for small groups began in first century Palestine and has continued on in one organic form or another as an unbroken heritage ever since. But let's be honest. Small groups started in the '80s. Or at least they began to catch on as a wider church culture phenomenon in the '80s.

This movement coincided with the emergence of the megachurch in America, which became a trendsetter and culture-creator for the wider church as it gained momentum and influence.

Small groups met a real practical need for megachurches. For generations, Sunday school had been the "other thing" that churches universally did. It worked well when you could offer 2 to 10 classes, depending on the size of your congregation, and comfortably accommodate everyone in the church.

But it becomes a real problem when you're trying to accommodate 3,000 people. You can build a 1,000 seat auditorium and offer three services to hold your main gathering, but that would translate to 100 to 125 classrooms! Talk about serious space issues. Not to mention resources, coordination, and programming. All of a sudden, Sunday school is a beached whale…unable to move, out of its natural environment, and a huge drain on the people trying to save it.

Decentralized, smaller gatherings of Christians in homes were the creative solution:

- They immediately solved the space conundrum by utilizing places that already existed but were lying unused by the church (living rooms).

- They solved the issue of coordination by placing the responsibility where it belonged in the first place—on the people who are the church.

- They simplified programming by offering one of two options: 1. Let the groups do their own thing. 2. Make the groups do the same thing.

Either way, problems resolved. The resources problem no longer existed because you didn't have to buy massive amounts of land to build huge campuses with tons of classroom space. No one had to constantly purchase or create Sunday school curriculums for 100 different classes on 100 different topics.

However, small groups weren't created for purely pragmatic reasons. Let's give our megachurch forefathers their due. If it were only for pragmatic reasons, the small groups trend would have never caught hold and spread through churches of all sizes. The original proponents of small groups found in them a true connection to the first century church and built them on a biblical foundation.

The most powerful reason why small groups gained momentum and continued to flourish, whether the originators acknowledge it or not, is because small groups filled the cultural chasm that existed between what people experienced on Sunday mornings and what they experienced throughout the rest of the week.

Playing Catch-Up

The caricature of the Sunday churchgoer in the 1980s was stuck in the 1950s. People still wore their Sunday finest and big smiles. There was a sense that church was very much just a part of what people did—part of the built-in routine and part of the social fabric. Church was a place where you could go and gain a sense of community with like-minded individuals.

And I imagine, for the most part, people probably did experience those things on Sunday mornings in the '80s.

However, there was a gigantic cultural shift between the 1950s and the 1980s. The '60s and '70s had been a tumultuous time of upheaval, revolution, and protest against the status quo. By the time the 1980s rolled around, a changing of the guard had come about. A new group of leaders had emerged to lead our nation and families. This group was a strange mix between the slightly older, who had actually participated in those social changes, and the children who grew up while those changes were going on. One thing is clear, though. In the 30-year time span between the '50s and the '80s, the old guard had faded and a new generation had stepped into the seats of power and influence.

What this emerging generation of adults was experiencing throughout their week was a world that looked and felt drastically different than it did in the '50s. The perception that we were going to figure out this whole life thing and ultimately find a happy ending evaporated in a puff of underlying postmodern philosophies and interactions with concrete reality. Not only could we see the problems that existed on a worldwide scale, but we were no longer certain we could really solve them.

Faith in the church as an institution began a downward spiral after televangelists like Jim Bakker and Jimmy Swaggart gained the trust of millions of Americans and then shattered it with scandal after scandal.

People no longer wore suits and dresses to work or social events. Culture had dressed down. Vocal unbelief and skepticism in church and religion was reaching an all-time high.

Throughout the '50s, the small town community was alive and well, even in the cities. Mom and pop businesses drove the local economy, and neighborhoods were filled with active stores, churches, and social clubs. As people moved out of the cities and into the suburbs, their homes were further away from where they worked, shopped, and went to church. They no longer rubbed shoulders and shook hands with the same people at the same social engagements. This is well-documented and discussed to the point of redundancy.

A void began to open up where community used to exist. By the time the 1980s rolled around, it wasn't merely a trend—it was the norm. Suburbia, with its scattered subdivisions and fenced-in yards, had fully replaced the localized neighborhood.

Accentuating this even more was television. TV had been around for a while, but by the '80s, television had been solidified as the number one source of entertainment for Americans, and it therefore became a cultural force. Once people began turning to TV for daily entertainment, they had even less motivation for going into their communities and interacting with real people.

All these factors converged to create a silo effect: Homes, with their privacy fences, big yards, and internal entertainment centers, housed people who were disconnected from the centers where they worked, shopped, and socialized. In addition, people no longer had unquestioning faith that church was the place to reliably find meaning, truth, and community.

Yet when people did go to church, it was all suits, smiles, and handshakes.

Groups to the Rescue

Into this gap stepped small groups. They provided a seemingly simple yet very important opportunity to connect the church to culture by having groups of Christians gather together in each other's homes. In this context, social interactions were theoretically more real and reflective of people's actual life experiences. Small groups filled the need for the sense of community that was missing in larger culture and provided a more grounded and authentic experience of Christian life.

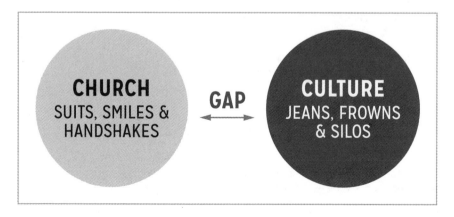

The living room seemed a perfect fit. By utilizing a place where people naturally gathered, Christians could live life together and see their faith lived out in practical ways. It was a place where community seemed familiar.

Small groups burst onto the scene as a revolutionary tour de force in how people experienced church. People could let their hair down, meet outside the church building, actually discuss faith and the Bible, and pray for each other—all in the comfy confines of their homes. They could wear normal clothes and sit in comfortable seats. And best of all, someone with the gift of hospitality always made good food to eat.

What Happens When They No Longer Fill the Gap?

So what are we getting at with all this talk about music, culture, and small groups? It's been more than 30 years since the emergence of small groups and, generally speaking, they still look and sound the same. Small groups are still playing 1980s Christian music.

That's right. We are playing Michael W. Smith and Petra in our small groups all across the nation. The gap between what the church is doing and how culture is trending has once again widened, and we are trying to fill it with outdated practices.

Have you listened to a Michael W. Smith song lately? Have you seen the music video for "I Love Rap Music" by DC Talk since the turn of the millennia? Whatever cultural gap they were filling in the late '80s and early '90s that allowed people to connect with the good news of Jesus Christ…that ship has sailed.

You say you still like Michael W. Smith and Petra? Very well and good. However, let's just be brutally honest—they are dated. The music scene has shifted. It's moved on. Sixteen to 25 year olds are not going to connect with 1980s contemporary Christian music. The phrase is an oxymoron anyway.

A couple of years ago, I attended the Catalyst Conference, a national conference designed for church leaders under the age of 40, and guess who made a guest appearance? Michael W. Smith. As 15,000 Christians worshiped together to Agneus Dei, it was like heaven on earth. We are well aware that worship isn't about the type of music (or music at all). What we are discussing here is connection—an analogy for the potential of connecting the Gospel message to an unbelieving world.

The mantle for relevant Christian music has passed to groups like Hillsong United and artists like Lacrae. The power of their music—and consequently their potential to contribute to the revival of the Christian message in popular culture and a Gospel movement among the emerging generation—is directly related to their position straddling the gap between what the church is doing and what is happening culturally.

When I think of our own church's contemporary, cutting-edge service playing Michael W. Smith or Petra, I imagine we would no longer be very cutting edge. Our services would probably be largely empty, save a core group of 40-somethings who really dig '80s Christian music.

In fact, if I can be excused to talk about One Life Church for just a moment— everything we do on Sunday mornings, from the parking lot to the lighting to the language used in the sermon, attempts to fill the cultural gap between what is perceived to be happening at church on Sunday mornings and what is actually happening outside the walls of the church the rest of the week. The preacher wears jeans. We create and use a lot of quality video. We play songs people hear on the radio. We do Projects (a service where we imagine *everyone* in the room is a skeptic or explorer). We practice and experiment with many more approaches. All of these practices are intended to connect with people where they're at.

This is not done to dilute the Gospel but to clear away all the noise that swallows up the message of the good news. It's done very intentionally and purposefully to fulfill the mission and vision of our church, which is to reach unchurched, secular-minded people and to help people far from God experience Jesus.

So why aren't we similarly intentional and purposeful about our small groups being on mission? How can we continue to allow them to lag behind as culture surges forward? Why are we still playing 1980s Christian music in our small groups?

How Do We Fill the Gap?

We opened this book with the cultural cows of small groups. We argued that the things we say are happening in our small group ministries—discipleship, authentic communities, a natural and invitational environment, living life together—are not actually happening. If we're honest with ourselves, the vast majority of our small group experiences are the exact opposite of the above ideal goals for how small groups operate.

However, acknowledging these cultural cows was not a negative attack on small groups or even the typical model for them. Just like I would never attack Michael W. Smith or Petra. It's merely an observation of reality. These very admirable goals for Christian community are not being accomplished in our small groups, because the model we use no longer fills the cultural gap it once did.

Another 30 years has gone by since the emergence of small groups. That's a long time. Yet another generation of leaders has emerged (or is currently emerging) to lead this nation. We have seen another revolution. While the '60s and '70s were a time of social revolution, we are currently in the midst of an information revolution. When new leaders arise and revolutions occur, paradigms shift. This naturally creates a new divide between church and culture. A divide in which, if we are not determined to engage, we temporal and contextual human messengers could miscommunicate the universal and timeless message of the Gospel.

In the next section, we would like to explore the three problems present in our culture and three corresponding paradigm shifts. These shifts need to occur in our small groups in order to fill the cultural gap and make clear the good news of Jesus Christ to the people who are our mission.

Problem #1: Loss of the Bible as the authoritative Word of God. The church says, "Accept the Bible." Culture says, "The Bible is irrelevant, unreliable, and dubious."

 Shift #1: From Bible study to creatively communicating the Gospel.

Problem #2: Invitational overload and loss of understanding of community. The church says, "Come do what we're doing." Culture says, "Come do what we're doing."

Shift #2: From invite to incarnationally invitational.

Problem #3: People are passionate about doing something, yet there is a void of meaning in and for people's lives. The church says, "Church is a worthy cause." Culture says, "There is a mass number of equally important causes."

Shift #3: From fellowship groups to mission teams.

Chapter 11

PARADIGM SHIFT #1: THE BIBLE SAYS

BY AUSTIN

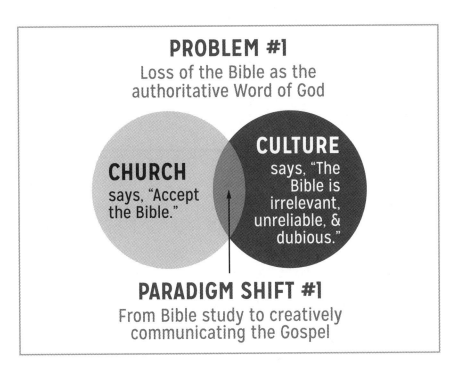

PROBLEM #1
Loss of the Bible as the
authoritative Word of God

CHURCH
says, "Accept
the Bible."

CULTURE
says, "The
Bible is
irrelevant,
unreliable, &
dubious."

PARADIGM SHIFT #1
From Bible study to creatively
communicating the Gospel

The Bible Says...Blah, Blah, Blah

There was a time when the phrase "the Bible says" tacked on the front of a statement used to carry some weight. Even among irreligious folk, "the Bible" still held a semblance of holiness and reverie. This isn't an old timer pining over the loss of the good ol' days; this is simply an acknowledgement that this is no longer the case. Consider these facts:

- 28 percent of practicing Christians and 16 percent of all adults "believe the Bible is the actual word of God and should be taken literally, word for word."[1]

- 38 percent of non-Christians under the age 35 view the Bible as inaccurate.[1]

- Of practicing Christians between the ages of 18 and 34, 18 percent say "the Bible, Quran, and Book of Mormon are all different expressions of the same spiritual truths."[1]

- Only 9 percent of American adults hold a biblical worldview.[2]

- 33 percent of Mosaics (currently the youngest generation) never read the Bible, and another 24 percent of Mosaics read the Bible only once a year.[3]

- 9 percent of Mosaics self identify as highly knowledgeable about the Bible, while 24 percent self identify as either not too knowledgeable or not at all knowledgeable about the Bible.[3]

> Mosaics are the generation born between 1984 and 2002. This generation is also sometimes referred to as the Millennials or Generation Y. Because of the data from David Kinnaman's book *You Lost Me: Why Young Christians Are Leaving Church...and Rethinking Faith*, or simply from plain observation, this generation is being referred to as the Prodigal generation within church circles due to the fact that they are leaving the church at an alarming rate.

The statistics are daunting, but personal experience is even more so. Remember the story that opened this book about my two friends who came to visit while I was in seminary? I mentioned we were able to dialogue about concerns, doubts, and skepticism they had concerning Christianity during the natural flow of living a normal day of life together. Well at one point I dropped the classic "the Bible says..." and that went over about as well as an Obama supporter at a Hank Williams Jr. concert.

> Be honest—what would be your immediate response to someone who came up to you and said "the Quran says..." in a way that was supposed to speak truth into your life? If we are going to be on mission, we need to reflect on how a person's foundation for belief affects *how* they hear.

What the comment did do was shift the direction of the conversation directly to the Bible, and my friend, who I respect as much or more than pretty much anyone in the world, said something I will literally never forget: "I hate the Bible."

I almost spit my drink across the table. Besides my friend speaking aloud what I thought was a set faux pas, I could not have been in a more diametrically opposed place in my life. I was falling in love with the Bible. Learning Greek and Hebrew, exegesis, history of hermeneutics, the metanarrative (big story) of Scripture—I was falling head over heels for the Bible. It was infusing my life with meaning, purpose, beauty, and love in ways I could have never foreseen.

My buddy's comment was a slap-in-the-face reminder of how people outside the faith community view the Bible. It was also a reminder of how I used to view the Bible myself, not that I ever would have said I hated it, but certainly that it held no relevance for my life and that it tended to create some seemingly negative consequences for people who took it too literally and adhered to it too closely.

My friend, on the other hand, was not only apathetic to the Bible, but he was vehemently opposed to it. Of course, through the course of the conversation I learned that he didn't truly hate the Bible itself—that would have been impossible since he had never given it a read, let alone a fair read. What he had such strong emotions about was people who used the Bible to uphold an opinion or stance that was against his and what he perceived it "did" to people.

From his perspective, there are social issues that need to be addressed, such as gay marriage and stem cell research, and these important issues cannot be advanced because a certain conservative crowd closes off the discussion wielding the Bible as the authoritative Word of God, which effectively slams the door shut. He does know the Bible never actually talks about gay marriage or stem cell research directly. What he *believes* is that people use the Bible to further their own stance on these issues.

What's more, he then flips on his preferred media outlet and sees Bible-thumping gay-haters picketing soldiers' funerals and fundamentalist groups proclaiming biblical judgment through terrorist acts on research labs.

Then he rubs up against individuals in conversation who uphold the Bible as the authority on an issue ("the Bible says..."), when in reality the Bible is not transforming every facet of these individuals' lives, nor is it seen in their everyday actions. Instead, they are exploiting the Bible to make their point stronger.

> Proof-texting is an interpretive method that takes a verse or passage without regard to its original intent and purpose and uses it to affirm a truth or principle in your life. While proof-texting is usually done with good intentions, it can be dangerous because God's Word should affect us and transform our lives, aligning us to God's will, rather than the other way around.

So I kind of relate to my friend's stance on the Bible, because often times when people say "the Bible says," whether with pure intentions or not, what they are actually communicating is, "This is the final word on the subject. Discussion closed."

The point here, believe it or not, is not to lambast Christians' interpretative methods. That is a different discussion. <u>The point is that simply saying "the Bible says" to a skeptical, unbelieving person, who does not hold the Bible to be the authoritative Word of God, not only carries zero weight, but it may actually close their ears to the biblical truths you are trying to communicate.</u>

That's in the Bible, Right?

The other haunting side of the coin is the Christian community itself. This is not scientifically verified data, simply my personal experience, but the vast majority of Christians I have met and talked openly with don't know exactly what to do with the Bible. They know they are supposed to be reading it. They have a desire to get to the place they know some people are—where the Bible is a very real and active part of their lives—however, they don't know how to go about reading it. There is confusion for them about what the Bible actually is.

They want someone, anyone, to explain the strange parts. What in the world are you supposed to do with the Old Testament? Can we kind of skip over those problematic passages we come across in our readings and focus on the ones we like and that line up with our beliefs?

Therefore, when these Christians say, "The Bible says...," it almost sounds like there should be a question mark at the end of their statement. They *think* that's what the Bible is saying, but at the end of the day they aren't so sure. That's not the sort of ringing endorsement an unbelieving world needs to hear from God's people.

There are also the Christians who are so unwaveringly sure of themselves that they amount to toddlers screaming "Lalalalala, I can't hear you!" with their fingers in their ears any time you try to engage them in an honest conversation about very important matters that deserve more attention.

What they are actually so unwaveringly sure of is that they are content with their lives and don't want anything or anyone, including the Bible and Jesus, to break into that contentment and challenge their beliefs.

There are also some self-professing Christians who don't truly know God at all, and they merely use his Word as a power play to position themselves into a higher worldly standing. We all wish this weren't so, but we all know it to be true.

These are three examples of Christian behavior along a very wide spectrum, from someone genuinely seeking out biblical truths but not knowing how to apply it to their lives to someone purposefully using the Bible as a tool to further a personal agenda.

My personal experience is that the scale is tipped extremely toward the good intentions side, but for anyone along the spectrum, the phrase "the Bible says" can be misunderstood or misused. Or both.

Small Group Bibles

Now, let's mentally transport ourselves to the classic small group setting. You have 12 people circled up and ready for discussion, Bibles open on their laps, and you've come to the "study" portion of group time. Statistics say that less than 2 of those 12 people hold a biblical worldview. That means the rest of the people in the room fit one of the following descriptions:

- They aren't exactly sure what to do with the Bible or are struggling through what the Bible is all about.

- They are the metaphorical child sticking their fingers in their ears the moment you begin speaking about biblical truths.

- They are marginal Christians (or Pharisees!) who are simply there to check off their Christian duty.

The product of the discussion during this study time inevitably deteriorates to, "What this passage means to me is...," which just happens to be the only phrase that will elicit a bigger eye roll from my unbelieving, skeptical buddy than "the Bible says..."

If you'll notice, who is not present in the discussion circle? The last place someone who verbalizes that they "hate the Bible" would willingly choose to be is in a circle of people talking about the Bible. Not high on their to-do list. This is at least a tad problematic, since we have pointed out that the church (gathered believers, aka small groups) are to be the body of Christ active in the world, and Jesus' mission was to seek and save the lost.

Modernism to Postmodernism

Adding to this rather tepid situation is the cultural milieu of the moment. Most people by now have heard the word postmodernism thrown around. Postmodernism is the philosophical move beyond modernism. Modernism can be best understood on the popular level as the sentiment that "we can figure it all out." Through collective and unified thought and action, we can accomplish anything. It was a grand narrative of the human spirit that believed humans, by human reason alone, could make all of humanity a better place.

Postmodernism arose out of the collapse of this surety. I have heard postmodernism expressed accurately as a mood opposed to a project. Think of it like this: Modernism is like construction workers erecting a building (the project), and postmodernism is the group of people wearing black hanging out on the corner smoking cigarettes wondering what the point is of all that hard work (the mood).

Renowned postmodern philosopher Jean-François Lyotard famously defined postmodernism as "incredulity toward metanarratives."[4] Simply meaning, our culture no longer believes there is one grand story (metanarrative) that tells the tale of humanity and gives us all a happy ending.

Here are a couple of examples that clearly display the "mood" of postmodernism, using modernism as it's illuminating counterpoint:

Modernism

Think: James Bond

- Just another number

- Driven by his mission

- Part of the machine

- Bent on one purpose

- Suit

- Technology and gadgets

- Fantastical

Postmodernism

Think: Jason Bourne

- Has to discover identity

- Driven by self-discovery

- Rebels against the machine

- Struggles with conscience

- Ragged, everyday clothes

- Hand-to-hand combat

- Realism

Modernism

Think: CSI

Very little facts or data given. It is up to the agents to sort through the facts and come up with the answer. In the end, they always come up with a solution and the good guy wins.

Postmodernism

Think: Lost

An abundance of facts are given but no real answers. Characters are forced to react to new data instead of figuring out any solution. At the end of each episode new questions are raised.

And surely you have heard the following statements made by people you know in your life or have at least heard on some TV show or another:

- "Whatever works for you..."

- "Who are you to judge me?"

- "Who's to say what's true?"

- "Whoever is in power sets the agenda."

- "People define who and what they are."

- "All religions point to the same place; all lead to God."

- "Whatever is considered right and wrong is based on the culture and society you grew up in."

Let's take a brief look at a few postmodern characteristics and show how they affect our current discussion on biblical authority.

From the Postmodern Worldview

- **Shift from confidence to suspicion.**[5] Pretty self-explanatory. People are no longer so certain the Bible is what it claims to be—or what other people claim it to be.

- **Social construction of reality.**[5] Truth was and is created by societies. So while the Bible might have worked for those people then, it is not a necessity for us now.

- **Violence and the therapy of deconstruction.**[5] This is the idea that all truth claims are moves to power, including ones in the Bible. If you say something is a certain way, it is because you are trying to rule or at least get the upper hand. However, we can find relief from the tyrannies of those in power by breaking down the claims they make. If you don't like the current authority, simply deconstruct what it holds to be true and erode its power.

- **Loss of language as explanatory.**[5] Maybe you've heard the ancient Eastern proverb of the turtles holding up the world. Postmodernism has shifted that metaphor to words. When you look up a word in the dictionary, what do you find? More words! Language itself can't explain everything because it's words all the way down.

An Eastern guru says to his followers, "The earth is supported on the back of an elephant." When asked what supports the elephant, he sagely responds, "It stands upon the back of a giant turtle." When asked, finally, what supports the giant turtle, he is briefly taken aback but quickly replies, "Ah, it is turtles all the way down."

- **Disorientation.**[5] Of course, once you are suspicious of everything, live in relativism, deconstruct all authority, and don't believe language can satisfactorily explain things, existence becomes a little disorienting. There is a void of meaning and purpose. Identity is called into question.

- **Hyper-reality and a culture of images.**[5] At the same time, we are bombarded with information and data through images. Just a couple years ago, it was declared that the world had shifted from a "text" world to a "visual" world. People no longer primarily communicate through the written word but instead communicate through images.

This cultural mood obviously has a huge impact on the view of the authority of Scripture and how both people inside and outside the faith community receive the Bible. If the general cultural mindset of our time is one that is naturally suspicious and creates a moving target for meaning, then a gap has been opened between the message the church has to deliver and the people who are the target audience.

The cultural gap that exists has the church on one side of the divide, saying you need to be reading the Bible as the authoritative Word of God, while the predominant message of popular culture on the other side of the divide is that all authority should be called into question and the Bible itself is historically unreliable, causing just as much harm as good. Anyone who has watched a History Channel documentary or follows any media outlet can feel this tension.

Poised and Ready

Small groups are perfectly poised to fill this gap, just as they were in the 1980s, with authenticity and community. But a simple move that actually becomes a huge paradigm shift for small groups is needed. Instead of thinking of group time as Bible study time, it should be used to creatively communicate the Gospel.

Anytime you mention a shift away from Bible study, there is a knee jerk reaction to go on the defensive. I completely understand. The hour I spend every morning studying in the original languages and digging into the exegetical process is consistently my favorite part of the day. When we started Lampstand Ministries (more on that later), I tried to launch it with an 8-week members' class, focused entirely on Christian doctrine. As I stated earlier in this book, I'm one of the last people who would devalue Bible study.

<u>However, just because we know we need to get Christians to study the Bible and we have small groups, does not necessarily mean the two should be wedded in bliss.</u>

Through their REVEAL study, Willow Creek Association has been conducting research about the spiritual life of Christians for more than a decade, having now collected half a million responses from 1,800 churches across a wide variety of denominations and geographical regions.[6] They found the number one mover of anyone toward a closer relationship with Jesus, regardless of where they are across the faith journey spectrum, is daily reflection on Scripture.[7]

What this means for groups is:

1. We should spur each other on in *daily* reflection of Scripture.

2. Group time itself should be the product of daily reflection of Scripture—not the replacement for it.

Let's continue to be brutally honest about what kind of small groups we have been promoting. How many times have you arrived at your weekly or biweekly group time knowing that everyone in your group (or even half!) has spent time reflecting on Scripture and is now ready to *study* it?

Or has it been much more frequent that the people in your group use the time to cross reflection, study, and discussion off their Christian to-do lists? Group time tends to stand in place of daily reflection, rather than being a supplement to it.

Are our groups falling under the classic idiom of insanity: "continuing to do the same activities while expecting different results"? Are our churches using small groups as the driving force for people to deepen their understanding of God's Word? When all the while the data returning to us over and over again is the same:

- Christians are not engaging with Scripture daily.

- Christians do not hold a biblical worldview.

- Christians confess to a lack of understanding of the Bible.

- Christians have a decreasing view of Scripture as the authoritative Word of God.

Breakthrough Thinking

It's sometimes good to do mental exercises when faced with a dilemma to create breakthrough thinking. If our goal is to see positive expressions of the above statements, then you might summarize it this way: A goal for the Christian community is to attain a deepening appreciation, relationship, and understanding of God's Word.

However, what if every Bible on the face of the earth were to simultaneously and instantaneously combust into ashes? Would the entire worldwide Christian community throw up their hands in exasperation, say "Welp, it was a good run, fellas," and then go on living as if Jesus wasn't through whom all things were made, move, and have their being?

I can imagine groups of Christians gathering to think of ways to creatively communicate the Gospel. They would no longer be able to hide behind the smokescreen of study in order to socialize. Instead, they would be forced to find ways to explain and show how the Gospel of Jesus Christ has transformed their lives. The purpose of the gathering would be more about sharing the good news than ostensibly building up the body.

Biblical Witness

At this point I have to turn to the biblical witness, as misplaced as it may seem at this point in my argument. Nonetheless, I'm going to drop a "the Bible says…"

Jesus was the master of creatively communicating the Gospel—using analogies, metaphors, and parables to connect eternal and infinite concepts to tangible, run-of-the-mill, real-life experiences (a farmer sowing seeds, leaven in flour, a mustard seed, a merchant looking for pearls, a net catching fish, a lost coin, a lost sheep, a lost son).

When Jesus spoke and taught, he got to the absolute truth of what he needed to get across by connecting that truth to real life experiences in a way that not only proclaimed the truthfulness of what he was relating, but also left the listener with the option to go back and explore the depths of the imagery. These messages were so successful that we are still pondering them 2,000 years later.

Jesus did not stop there. His creative communication of the Gospel did not end with parables but was also grounded in physical expression: the woman at the well, Zacchaeus in the tree, the adulterous woman, the rich young ruler, and many others.

I'm not talking about object lessons, although Jesus was certainly the master of those too, but rather seeing the good news alive or missing from the actions of a person and linking that to the real life experiences people were living through.

The black and white reality is that everyone is either living under grace or not. There are endless opportunities to reveal the goodness of God as lived out through our interactions with other people. Jesus, of course, modeled this deftly.

Besides verbal and physical communication, Jesus also used miracles to creatively communicate the Gospel—wine at the wedding feast, the multitude of healings, calming the storm, the feeding of the 5,000. And this is just a sampling of the miraculous.

This is about as creative as it gets! If only we could control weather and produce something from nothing, we would probably get an A+ on our creative communication of the Gospel report card. It would be a mistake to write off Jesus' miracles because they were done by Jesus and can only be replicated by him or to take the other extreme of thinking that every Christ-follower should begin praying for the power to do miracles in their small groups. The purpose of the miracles done by Jesus fit into two very broad categories:

1. To reveal the glory of God and the coming of his kingdom.

2. To enact life transformation.

Really these purposes are one and the same. We will look later at what these two might look like expressed through small groups, but for now, I will just say that we live every day in the reality of the first purpose. God's glory has been revealed; his kingdom has come. And for those of us who have experienced regeneration and newness of life through Jesus Christ, we can give firsthand testimony to the miracle of the second purpose—enacting life transformation. Don't be quick to pass off the miraculous as an unattainable resource for our groups.

Apostles' Witness

When you turn the pages of the Bible past the Gospels and get into the witness of the apostles, you get more creative communication of the good news. Peter uses the Old Testament to point to Jesus as the Messiah (which at that time and to that audience was creative indeed), and then there's the famous example of Paul's sermon on Mars Hill. Move to the epistles, and you find them chock-full of analogies, metaphors, and tangible examples of the good news of Jesus Christ being related to those in the first century church. And the book of Revelation may be the most creative of them all.

No Better Model

When you really think about it, the entire New Testament is one long creative communication of the Gospel. Why? Because the people who comprised the New Testament didn't have a Bible! At least, not the New Testament. When Paul went out to plant a church, all he had was the Old Testament, the historical event of Jesus Christ, and the life experiences of himself and his team. What he and the other New Testament authors did over and over again was use those tools in creative ways to connect the message of Jesus Christ to their audience. This is why none of the New Testament books read like a textbook that we can "study" and give correct exam answers to in order to receive a passing grade...which, coincidentally, could have saved us thousands of years of theological deliberation and debate.

The New Testament books don't read like that because that was not and is not their purpose. The writers were simply sharing the *new* good news.

This is very familiar to us today—the whole idea of using Scripture, the historical event of Jesus, and life experiences to creatively communicate the Gospel. It is exactly what preachers do every Sunday. The difference between what a preacher does and what happens in groups is that preachers actually deliver the message to an audience. Their study has purpose, focus, and urgency, knowing that it will be received.

That is exactly the shift that needs to take place in our small groups. They need to get focused, gain purpose, and feel urgency by delivering the Christian message with the expectation that it will be received. However, not all of us are gifted orators, nor should all of us be giving 20 to 30 minute teachings on various theological, interpretive, and pastoral topics. Here's where the creative part comes in.

People are naturally creative because they are made in the image of the Creator. Within each of us is an artist, but our artistry takes different forms and will produce vastly different works of art. Yet, more than anything, we want to use what's inside of us. I love this quote by Erwin McManus:

> Though there has never been one ordinary human being born, it's amazing how most of us end up living ordinary lives. How is it that with our first breath we could be so extraordinary, but with our last breath we could die so ordinary?[8]

McManus calls upon the church to reclaim its rightful spot as the epicenter of human creativity. To be the liberators of humanity. Our job is to call people out of their ordinary lives and into their created intent of having an extraordinary relationship with their Creator. This is the heart of the paradigm shift we are calling for in our small groups. Bible study needs to happen, but we are asking the church to tap into its potential and liberate the communities they are involved in by creatively communicating the Gospel to the people in those communities.

Here are just a few benefits of buying into this paradigm shift and beginning to creatively communicate the Gospel in our small groups. This is how we utilize our perfectly positioned groups to close the cultural gap.

On One Side You Have the Church

Creatively communicating the Gospel...

- **Forces us to know the story.** Not all of us can have seminary degrees. Not even all of our small group leaders can have seminary degrees. What's more, there's a good chance the vast majority of the people in our churches will never become completely comfortable with the book of Habakkuk. <u>But we have to get to the place where our churches are full of people who know the big story of God's redemptive acts, are able to communicate them, and feel comfortable doing so.</u> If week in and week out we are creatively communicating the Gospel, there will be no choice but to know the narrative of God's love for us.

- **Returns every group time to Jesus.** In a Twitter post on September 23, 2012, Ed Stetzer (@edstetzer) said: "Don't preach or teach a message that would still be true if Jesus hadn't died on the cross." How many of our group times go by without a mention of the Gospel or even of Jesus Christ? I'll admit that I'm guilty of this as a group leader sometimes. Crazy! Jesus is the sum and total of all things through whom all things hold together, move, and have their being! How can we not tap into this during our group times? If we are creatively communicating the Gospel in our groups, then we will be returning to Jesus as the source.

- **Creates ownership of the group.** There is an unhealthy expectation for group leaders in small groups. It needs to end. I believe in leadership, so I think small groups should have leaders. However, the actual group time itself has to be owned by the group. All group members need to be invested in making the group time happen. For the whole group to consistently and creatively communicate the Gospel, everyone will need to contribute to the creative process. All will have to contribute or it won't happen. And then at least you know why your group is failing and it won't fall on the shoulders of an overburdened, under-resourced leader who was unnecessarily and unfairly expected to do more.

- **Necessarily turns the focus outward.** Even if you never actually deliver the message as a group (which would be a shame), mentally you are forced to think outside the group. We have to break our Christian huddle and get outside our living rooms. A catalyst for making this happen is to envision and create opportunities where your group creatively communicates the Gospel.

On the Other Side You Have the Culture

Creatively communicating the Gospel...

- **Removes the phrase "the Bible says" and infuses "Scripture is."** To an audience who does not hold the Bible as the authoritative Word of God, living out the good news of Jesus Christ may be the only possible chance for us to show them what Scripture actually is. We have to transform our lives into a holistic biblical worldview so that God's Word is not something we beat somebody over the head with, but rather something that becomes incarnate in our actions. Creatively communicating the Gospel allows us to stand astride the cultural gap, never having to proclaim what the Bible says to those outside the faith community, and yet they can have no questions whatsoever about how Scripture brings life.

- **Compellingly tells a "little story."** The interesting and paradoxical part of the postmodern mood is that while it holds an "incredulity towards metanarratives," it leaves open the possibility for sharing a "mete-narrative," or small story. When you remove all the "grand narratives" from life, you also lose the overarching meaning and purpose of life. There is a vacuum created where those things once belonged. We have a culture that has deconstructed itself into meaninglessness. People don't stay in meaninglessness long; it doesn't "fit." Creatively communicating the Gospel can fill the void by telling the "big story" of Scripture in small ways. The Gospel has proven to transcend time, culture, and geography. As believers in God's Word, we know it to be a true reflection of all reality, but the compelling truth is that it is nonetheless true for each individual experience.

- **Is done by real people, who are harder to hate.** Anyone can hate a caricature. There is the atheist caricature of Christians as Bible-toting dullards, who blindly accept truths from a "higher power" that ends up looking a lot like the God in the mirror. There is the Christian caricature of atheists as having devil horns, who are creating this vast conspiracy to purposefully undermine God and the church. Then there is the vast majority of "everyday people" who love to point at both extremes and say, "At least I'm not one of those crazies," so that they can continue living a comfortable, unexamined life. One of the necessities of creatively communicating the Gospel is proximity. Caricatures break down through relationships. While someone might be vehemently opposed to the Bible, they might be open to a conversation with their Bible-believing friend at a pub over some things the Bible has to say.

- **Makes use of all available resources.** Remember the resources Paul had when going to plant a church: the Old Testament, the historical event of Jesus Christ, and his life experiences. The truth is, he had a couple other resources as well. He had a team, and he had the people he was trying to reach. When we creatively communicate the Gospel in our small groups, we are utilizing an important aspect—our team (groups)—but we are also utilizing the most important resource that largely gets overlooked, and that is the people far from God themselves! Paul said to the Athenians, "I am not here to tell you about a strange foreign deity, but about this One whom you already worship, though without full knowledge" (Acts 17:23, *The Voice*). God's existence is not contingent on our ability to explain or prove him; he is already manifest in all facets of our culture. God is a reality to all people's experience, because God is reality. All we have to do is help to reveal what is already present!

Conclusion

We're living in the middle of an information revolution. The average person receives more data in one day than our forefathers used to get in a lifetime. For all the advances in our gadgets, gizmos, and the next greatest electronic device, they are only tools to get at the greatest advancement available to us—the sharing and receiving of heretofore unfathomable amounts of data.

Churches, while late to the game, are making some advancement in using this information revolution to further the kingdom. YouVersion Bible app is a great tool. Broadcasting especially gifted and ordained teachers is another. The amazing thing is that while available resources for understanding the Bible are at an all-time high, Christians, as a collective community, continue in the downward trend of apprehension and not holding a biblical worldview.

I believe this is because we are not capitalizing on our best available resource. Depending on how you look at it, there is somewhere between 2 billion and 2.8 billion professing Christians in the world. Billion! Imagine all of them gathering in small groups with the purpose of creatively communicating the Gospel to people who do not know the message of Jesus Christ.

Do you know who I have found to be the best studiers of the Bible? People who are madly and wildly in love with God. And the people who are madly and wildly in love with God are the people who have truly experienced Jesus. By shifting the paradigm of our small groups away from Bible study toward creatively communicating the Gospel, we make the product of our group time to be Jesus.

Chapter 12

PARADIGM SHIFT #2: INVITE TO INCARNATIONALLY INVITATIONAL

BY AUSTIN AND ZACH

PROBLEM #2
Invitational overload and loss
of understanding of community

CHURCH
says, "Come
do what
we're doing."

CULTURE
says, "Come
do what
we're doing."

PARADIGM SHIFT #2
Invite to incarnationally invitational

Generation One

A couple months ago, my brother-in-law and I were sharing stories from our high school and college days. I was joking about the giant "Zach Morris style" cellphone that I carried in high school (forgive me if you're too young for a *Saved by the Bell* reference). It was about 5 inches thick, and you had to pull up the antenna every time you wanted to talk to someone. It was a small step up from a car bag phone.

It wasn't just the phone that was inconvenient; the cellphone plans were as confusing as a Jackson Pollock painting. There were no nationwide plans. Anyone who had a cellphone at that time was terrified to actually use it. In my town, there was an 80 percent chance that the highways were covered on your plan, but if you were on the back roads, you were "roaming" and it would cost you a million dollars a second. I still had to buy those prepaid phone cards when I went to college because I never knew if my cellphone was going to work or not.

Throughout the conversation, my brother-in-law told me a shocking secret...cellphones weren't around when he was in high school or college. *What?* For the last 10 years, my cellphone has been a constant (sometimes constant annoyance) in my life. I sort of forgot that there was a time before cellphones. I remember saying, "How did you ever make plans or connect with anyone?"

He informed me that he would use his home phone to call someone on their home phone. If they were going to do anything, they had to lay out exactly where they were going, who was coming, and what time they were leaving. If they were already out and you were looking for them, well, that was just too bad. If you weren't invited from the start, then you weren't going to be able to join the party unless you just got lucky and found them.

Even though that was less than 20 years ago, it seems light-years in the past. It has never been easier to communicate than it is right now. Tomorrow, we could make the same statement. And again next week, and again next year. Each day technology moves forward and is constantly finding new ways to speed up communication.

Generation Two

For Davin, my 15-year-old nephew, the home phone is an antique. Much like how my grandmother's rotary phone was an antique to me when I was 15. Davin has never crowded around a home answering machine with his family and made a silly outgoing message. He has never been out and about with no way to get a hold of someone, never used a payphone, and if I broke out an old car bag phone it would blow his mind.

For Davin, communication is and always has been instant. His cellphone is never far from him. With the touch of a button, he can text 20 friends at the same time. When he plays video games, he wears a headset and teams up with people all over the world. To him, the world is small. The world is reachable. After all, China is a simple connection away. He can communicate with anyone, anywhere, instantly. If he can't get a hold of someone, he has text, Facebook, Twitter, Foursquare, email, and a number of other options to track them down. He has the ability to have ongoing conversations without actually saying an audible word.

A New Reality in Community

Whether we realize it or not, the availability, speed, and ease of communication changes the way we think. It changes what we do and how we react. Like everything, it has a cause/effect relationship, and it creates ripples in the ways we operate.

One of the ripples that the advancements in ease and speed of communication have caused is that it has redefined community. This new community is radically different from the one in the 1980s when small groups emerged. Now email, instant messaging, chat rooms, blogs, MySpace, Facebook, Twitter, and whatever comes next are the tools that shape and define our current understanding of community. People can like what they want, join what they want, get LinkedIn, make a page, a group, a following—in other words, they have the ability and freedom to create their own social networks in a way that vastly supersedes all potential capabilities that were present even 5 years ago.

Author and marketing guru Seth Godin would argue that even the word *community* is antiquated. He suggests that we have broken our lives into subsets of like-minded "tribes."[1] Over here you have the tribe you play real sports with; over there is the tribe you play fantasy sports with. You have your church tribe, parenting tribe, work tribe, toastmasters tribe—depending on your personal stamina, charisma, and social acumen, you can belong to as many (or few) tribes as you'd like.

These tribes are focused groups. The tribes gather for a specific reason to accomplish specific social goals. In fact, it's not kosher to bring too much of one tribal topic into another tribe. The fantasy sports tribe (as a whole anyway) does not want to hear about parenting, and the work tribe doesn't want to hear much about how awesome your victory was in fantasy football last week. These tribes are mutually exclusive.

Invitation Overload

While the ripple of redefined community occurs at more of a macro level, the second ripple caused by the speed and ease of communication shows itself on the micro, personal level. With the unprecedented explosion of available tribes, there is a continual opportunity to join just about everything. The effect is a phenomenon known as "invitation overload."

Back in September 2012, Mark Zuckerberg went on the Today Show and announced that the number of active Facebook users had reached 1 billion. As shocking as that stat is, what is more shocking is that I'm pretty sure I have received an invite to play Farmville, Mob Wars, or Bejeweled from at least half those users.

As I look through my Facebook notifications from the past 48 hours, I see three different invites to a concert in Nashville, one in Canada, an invite to an *Extreme Makeover Home Edition* watching party in Knoxville, an invite to a poker tournament in Evansville, two invites to Tupperware/holiday parties from people I don't know, and over twelve invites to like various companies, artists, and organizations.

We have become an invitation culture. Whether virtual or in person, we operate in groups. If we are going somewhere, we invite. The invite itself actually holds very little weight; accept or blow off—it doesn't really make a difference. In this redefined community, full of invitation overload, the invitation simply becomes an extension of who we are and our need to exist in groups rather than an intentional pursuit of relationship. The invite is simply a product of living in an invitation culture, and invitation overload is coming from all directions.

No Room to Join Anything

Invitation overload can have a paralyzing effect. The problem is that we want to do it all, think we can do it all, and eventually become so overwhelmed that we can't effectively do anything. Our fast-paced, fill-every-second-with-one-stimuli-or-another lifestyles are well documented. There is no need to try to prove it exists; just do a quick look at your week.

There are times I look at my calendar and think, "How did this day end up looking like this!?" After accounting for work, family, bills, groceries, little league, and school plays, we are left with time and energy for little else. But outside those things we still have to make time for friends, family, service, adventure, and basic social interaction.

A few weeks ago, my wife and I had so much going on during the week that we had to cancel an invitation from my sister. What's really sad is that the invitation was simply to come over and eat pizza at her house. I asked my wife, "When did eating free pizza become so stressful?" Our busy schedules can leave us paralyzed, unable to do anything, and wondering what to choose.

Never Fully Present

It is becoming increasingly difficult to ever be fully present in our culture. If the already high demands on our time are not enough, we have now given everyone a handheld attention-deficit creator: live Facebook and Twitter feeds in the palm of your hand. You can receive instant notifications that vibrate and flash, drawing your immediate attention away from wherever you are and whatever you're doing. People are constantly being pulled into one tribe, even as they are trying to be present in another.

This is not a negative assessment of the situation; it is a commentary on the reality of it. I have watched as meetings (even one-on-one), parties, and even small groups have turned into phone gazing gatherings.

All this comes together to declare one loud message: You are too busy!

We Have a Program for That

Bill Gates is quoted as saying, "Just in terms of allocation of time resources, religion is not very efficient. There's a lot more I could be doing on a Sunday morning."[2]

Honestly, I get it. Obviously I would never give up my relationship with Christ or my commitment to his local church, but the church is a major contributor to invitation overload, and it has a significant impact on what we can and can't do. However, the countless ongoing invitations that the church extends parade around with a different, more positive name—programming.

Church programming is simply all the different activities that members of a church can choose to participate in—and they can be overwhelming.

I did a quick Google search of "Christian church calendars" and pulled up one of the first links. The church had an event/programming calendar so everyone could see what all they could be a part of.

Let's start with Sunday and see what we can do.

8:30, 9:30, or 10:30AM Worship Service (If you are serving you will need to be at all 3 services.)	**SUNDAY**
4:00PM Choir Rehearsal	
5:00PM Youth Groups/Adult Study	

9:00AM Keenagers Meeting 5:00PM Small Groups 6:00PM Curriculum Meeting	**MONDAY**
6:00AM Book Club 8:15AM Fellowship Basketball 5:00PM Small Groups	**TUESDAY**
5:00PM Fellowship Meal 6:00PM Youth Group 6:00PM Adult Programming	**WEDNESDAY**
9:00AM Ladies' Bible Study 5:30PM 1st Service Practice 6:15PM 2nd Service Practice 6:30PM Financial Peace University	**THURSDAY**
Day Off	**FRIDAY**
7:00AM Church-Wide Rummage Sale 9:00AM Men's Prayer Breakfast	**SATURDAY**

This does not include the endless offers of kids and athletic activities that many churches offer. It doesn't include the softball leagues, basketball leagues, VBS planning, prayer team meetings, Bible Bowl, etc., etc.

Programming can get away from even time-conscious churches. I know the church I attend is conscious of how much programming they offer, because they have a deep desire for people to be active in the community. They say no to a lot more than they say yes to when it comes to programming.

Still, there are weeks when I have life group, core meetings, worship practice, and planning meetings, and before I know it I only have one open night, and it has to be earmarked for family if I wish to stay married. Which I do.

The problem is, we are being given conflicting messages that set us up for failure. On the one hand, we are quoted "The Great Commission" and being told to get out in the community, surround ourselves with people far from God, and "make disciples." On the other hand, the church is programming away the small amount of free time we have. If we are successful at one, we are likely going to fail at the other.

Keeping Tabs

Sometimes we get involved in areas of church programming for the wrong reasons. No one would audibly say it, but oftentimes church members and leaders give off the vibe that attendance at church programming directly correlates with how much you love Jesus. This leads to people feeling pressure that they have to be at everything the church offers if they are going to be considered a "good Christian."

Church leaders say encouraging things like, "That guy is really committed to the church. He is involved in everything." The pressure can leave you feeling guilty if you skip a fellowship meal to go watch a basketball game with a co-worker.

When I was in youth ministry, I remember parents making their children miss playing in their community sponsored all-star baseball games if they ever fell on a Sunday or Wednesday.

The message is that church invitation trumps all. From an early age, we set into the minds of our children the idea that church programming is the top of the pyramid, and every other invitation can only be accepted if there is no conflict. So we choose Upward Basketball instead of local community leagues. We choose Bible Bowl over an academic club at school. Even as adults we choose church leagues over rec leagues. And instead of being visible and available to the community, the lovers of Jesus in our towns and churches are tied up in church programming. The reality is that many churches are programming themselves right out of their mission.

The church is saying, "Get involved in the community! As long as it doesn't interfere with the prayer breakfast."

Made Aware

So culture is saying, "Come do what we're doing," and the church is saying, "Come do what we're doing, but make sure you are doing what they're doing too."

The reality is that every time you say yes to one thing, you say no to something else.

Every time I say yes to worship practice on Thursday night, I am saying no to a group of non-church guys who play basketball at a local gym and then go to a local sports bar to watch the Thursday night NFL game.

In church culture the always expanding invites, or programming, keep us focused inward and living in a bubble. While church programming can play a vital role in church development, our churches should communicate the true mission and verbalize that community invites trump church programming.

How do we bridge the gap between what culture is saying and what the church is doing? The answer leads us to a popular church program from the '80s and '90s.

Paradigm Shift—Incarnationally Invitational

Do you remember "Bring-a-Friend Sunday"? I'm not really sure the reach of this event or if churches still actively participate today, but I remember it well growing up. Right next to a terrible clipart picture of a Bible or two friends laughing would be the headline: "Next Week is Bring-a-Friend Sunday." It was the one day to be intentionally evangelistic. There was nothing really special about this day. The service didn't change; the message didn't change. You could simply throw a dart at the calendar and whatever day it landed on could hold the honor of being "Bring-a-Friend Sunday."

It was the most basic of challenges: Simply invite someone. You don't have to give the Gospel message; you don't even have to sit with the person. All you have to do is give the invite. The message of the church was clear: "You get them here, and we'll do the rest."

While our lives as Christians would be a little simpler if that were the case, statistics tell us that "You get them here, and we'll do the rest" is not a successful model of evangelism. According to research done by Barna Group, there are 3,500 to 4,000 churches that close their doors each year in America alone. Furthermore, churches lose an estimated 2,765,000 people each year to nominalism and secularism.[3]

If the church is ever going to make a dent in the number of people abandoning ship, it must be anchored in relationships. It must be anchored in people opening up their lives to people far from God and letting those people walk alongside them in faith.

The opposite is true as well. If we are tied down to endless church programming and we are not making relationships outside the church, those numbers will continue to bottom out at alarming rates.

Standing in the gap between what culture is saying and what the church is doing is the shift toward becoming incarnationally invitational. To break it down to its simplest form, incarnation means to be the embodiment of something. So to be incarnationally invitational is to allow your life to embody invitation, to extend your life out to others at all times, and to be at the very core of who you are an invitation.

Jesus: The Model of Incarnational Invitation

Incarnate means to take a quality or idea and embody it. To give it concrete form. When theologians and church leaders talk about Jesus being God Incarnate, they are saying that Jesus embodies all of God while living the flesh and blood life that we experience. Fully God. Fully man. This is heady stuff. Good stuff to think about, though, because it reveals the depth and beauty of God, both who he is and his love for us.

One of the things that helps me wrap my mind around "God Incarnate" is to look at the life of Jesus and see him live out the characteristics of God in ways that transcend normal human behavior. We can love others, but Jesus is Love. We can do good deeds, but Jesus is Goodness. We can comfort others, but Jesus is Healing. Jesus does not merely personify an abstract idea of how we feel godly people should act; Jesus actually embodies the fullness of God while being a person.

Jesus was present. There are two aspects of Jesus' life that don't get nearly enough attention in my opinion: that he was born at all and that he ascended.

Hebrews tells us that Jesus can sympathize with our weaknesses because he was tempted in all things. This includes being a baby, going through puberty, and coming of age, among others. On the complete opposite side of the spectrum, through the power of God, Jesus did something we cannot relate to at all. He ascended to the right hand of the Father to reign over the kingdom of God for eternity and is actively perfecting his people for all time.

Jesus being present in these two ways is utterly unfathomable to us for two very different reasons:

1. Because it is so practical (Jesus lived a real life).

2. Because it is so far beyond our experience or explanation (Jesus continues to reign).

This dynamic was what made Jesus' life so revolutionary; he *is* the presence of God *in* the presence of his people.

Possibly the four greatest phrases in the Gospels are "now when" in Matthew, "immediately" in Mark, "now it happened" in Luke, and "after these things" in John. These transition phrases marked the movement of Jesus into new areas, regions, and communities, which truly marked the presence of God in the lives of real people. Wherever these movements took him, God's Word was taught and healings occurred. Jesus "suffered" through interruptions, requests, accusations, and a generally chaotic existence, because everywhere he was, is where he was supposed to be. He was fully present.

Jesus was magnetic. It's really unexplainable where the popular caricature of Jesus as the lone figure, or small-time teacher with only a few followers, came from. That is just not the picture presented in the Gospels. What we get is the image of a completely magnetic figure in every sense of the word.

Jesus simply says, "Follow me," and these everyday people do just that. It is incredible, so incredible in fact that most modern scholars believe Jesus had a preexisting relationship with at least Peter, Andrew, James, and John. As remarkable as it is for someone to get a complete stranger to drop everything and follow them through life, I think it is even more remarkable for that to happen between people who already know each other.

Could you imagine going up to one of your friends at their workplace and saying, "Follow me"? What would their reaction be? Especially since the first century Jewish person would have heard, "Follow me, and I will be your teacher in life in the ways of God." Laughter would probably be the number one response from my friends.

> When Jesus spoke the words "Follow me," he flipped the cultural protocol for the rabbi/ disciple relationship on its head. Typically, the would-be disciple would cast his lot with a rabbi. He would approach the teacher, and if the teacher accepted the request, the disciple would submit to the authority of the rabbi in all things. You asked the rabbi; the rabbi didn't ask you.

Jesus' magnetism extended beyond his immediate followers. The Gospels relate time and time again that wherever Jesus went a crowd was soon to appear. This wasn't only a localized movement. People came from all over: Galilee, Judea, Jerusalem, Idumea, beyond the Jordan, Tyre, and Sidon. That's like pulling people from all over the United States with all their differences (think New Yorker vs. Texan vs. Seattleite vs. Southerner) as well as from Mexico and Canada. These were people with vastly different worldviews, political ideologies and affiliations, ethnicities, and religious backgrounds all drawn to the same person.

Even when the crowd seemed to be an obstruction to where he was going and what he was doing, Jesus stops to receive them and share with them the message of the good news of the kingdom of God. This unquestioned openness and availability drew crowds of people.

As a testament to his true magnetism, Jesus even drew his "enemies" to himself. For every story of a potential follower coming to Jesus, there is a story of someone who is antagonistic or outright hostile approaching him as well. Those poor whipping boys, the Scribes and Pharisees, just couldn't stay away! Yet, Jesus receives them too. While never backing down from the truth, he engaged them in an ongoing dialogue that allowed people who didn't believe what he was saying or doing to return and experience him more.

Jesus was intentional. While Jesus was present in all situations and drew everyone in, he was also very intentional about the relationships he developed. The fact that out of the crowds there were disciples, and out of the disciples there were 12 named, and out of the 12 there was the "inner circle," is proof that he poured into people in intentional ways.

Jesus also sought out particular people to befriend like Lazarus, Mary, Martha, and Nicodemus. We see that he went out of his way to intervene in the lives of individuals like the woman at the well and Zacchaeus in the tree.

While there was a general openness and availability to his life, for some there was also a direct invitation *into* his life. We don't always get to see the reason why Jesus chose to be intentional toward a specific person and not another, but when we do, the result was to extend the invitation to know him in an exponential way. Through the woman at the well, the whole Samaritan town accepted the invitation to come and see, and through Zacchaeus countless people got to see the power of Jesus through life transformation.

Jesus was all in. As you look at Jesus' interactions with people, you quickly realize there is no situation he would not step into: Touch an unclean man—check. Talk with an outcast woman with a bad reputation—check. Cross over into hostile political areas—check. Hang out at parties with people of ill repute—check. Teach controversial messages to religious people in their places of worship—check. Accept praise and adoration while riding a donkey—check.

Three of my favorite situations Jesus gets into by living an incarnationally invitational life are the calling of Matthew, Zacchaeus in the tree, and dinners with the Pharisees.

With Matthew, it's one of the classic "Follow Me" stories. As is true with all of Jesus' invitations (the exception being the young ruler), Matthew drops everything in order to follow him. It's interesting that the first thing Jesus did was follow Matthew to his home. Matthew wanted to celebrate his life change, but more than that he wanted to celebrate the source of his life change. He didn't know the rules; he just called up his buddies, fellow tax collectors and sinners, and threw a party for Jesus. In what had the potential to be a pretty awkward situation, surrounded by the most hated men in society, Jesus was right at home. When the inevitable criticisms come from the religious vanguard, what does Jesus say? He looks around at his new friends and loved ones and says, *These are who I have come for.*

With Zacchaeus, Jesus invites himself over! I love the moxie of Jesus in this story. It also highlights all the points we've made so far. Jesus was present in Jericho. He was incredibly magnetic, drawing a crowd by simply passing through the town, and caused this stranger to climb a tree just to catch a glimpse of him. He was intentional, going straight up to the tree where Zacchaeus was and engaging him in conversation, and he apparently had no hesitation in inviting himself right into Zacchaeus' home and life. Zacchaeus wasn't just any tax collector—he was a chief tax collector. This meant he took percentages of money from the other tax collectors and was therefore most likely hated by the men who were themselves the most hated people in society. By publicly inviting himself to the home of this man, Jesus was asking for heated glares and criticism, which he got. But he only had eyes for Zacchaeus. As Zacchaeus turned to Jesus and said, "I will give half my wealth to the poor, Lord, and if I have cheated people on their taxes, I will give them back four times as much!" Jesus in turn looked to his detractors and said, *This is who I have come for* (Luke 19:8).

Twice in Luke, Jesus accepts an invitation from the Pharisees, the religious leaders who would eventually conspire to have him murdered. Jesus ups the moxie level a couple notches in these stories as he directly challenges their way of life. At first glance, this may seem rude; he accepts their invitation and then turns around and lambasts them. However, sometimes the greatest show of compassion you can give someone is to challenge them and not allow them to continue down a path of destruction.

In these two stories, Jesus tells multiple parables, letting these religious leaders know they are missing the mark. They have not been given their positions of influence and power for self-edification but to build up and save "the poor, the crippled, the lame, and the blind" (Luke 14:13). They have been brought close to God so that they can help those far from God experience him. In challenging them in this way, Jesus was actually looking around the table at those he also loved and foreshadowing his words on the cross— "Father forgive them..." (Luke 23:34). He was saying, *Yes, even for you I have come.*

Application

Hopefully by now the application points are clear. In a sermon I heard a few years ago, the pastor told a story of a man who came up to him after a particular service and said something along the lines of: *That was a good sermon and everything, but really anyone could do what you did. You just opened up the Bible, read some verses, and said, "C'mon guys, just do what it says here!"*

We say we are Christ-followers, but we rarely take the time to explore Christ's life and try to apply his actions in our everyday life. When applying a shift toward a life that is incarnationally invitational, I kind of just want to say to group leaders and group members, "C'mon guys! Can't you see what it says here? Just do it! Imagine the impact!"

Of course, it is not that easy. You have to truly know Christ and understand the Gospel to be motivated to reflect Christ. For our groups to be present, magnetic, intentional, and all in, we have to first be a people who draw our ultimate sustenance from the Gospel.

Titus 3:4-7

[4] When God our Savior revealed his kindness and love, he saved us, [5] not because of the righteous things we had done, but because of his mercy. He washed away our sins, giving us a new birth and new life through the Holy Spirit. [6] He generously poured out the Spirit upon us through Jesus Christ our Savior. [7] Because of his grace he declared us righteous and gave us confidence that we will inherit eternal life.

When we truly understand that this Scripture, Titus 3:4-7, is truth—that mercy, freedom, and rescue is our standing before God and the reality of our existence—then we don't do service projects once a quarter in order to cross it off our checklist of being a dynamic small group. Instead, we are embodying Christ in our communities.

Titus 3:1-2, 8

[1] Remind the believers to submit to the government and its officers. They should be obedient, always ready to do what is good. [2] They must not slander anyone and must avoid quarreling. Instead, they should be gentle and show true humility to everyone. [8] This is a trustworthy saying, and I want you to insist on these teachings so that all who trust in God will devote themselves to doing good. These teachings are good and beneficial for everyone.

<u>We are embodying the invitation for others to come see Christ with our very lives. In this way, we transcend merely an invite to do one more thing—we actually become a gift.</u> As we become present in all situations, seeing that where we are is where we are supposed to be, becoming radically open to all people in all situations while intentionally engaging a select few on a deeper level, and being ready to step into any circumstance—in other words, to live a lifestyle that is incarnationally invitational—our groups won't be just another thing we have to do, competing in an already demanding culture. Instead, they will be an invitation to experience the One who is worthy and receives all glory, honor, and praise.

"The Invite" vs. "Incarnationally Invitational"

There is a fundamental difference between being a serial inviter and being incarnationally invitational. While I'm sure there are many more, we have identified seven truths of being incarnationally invitational.

1. Being incarnationally invitational means a long-term investment in people. "The Invite" says, "I've got an open night, let's fill it with something. Do you want to go to a movie?" An incarnational invitation says, "You can call me anytime, my door is always open for you." To accept the challenge of being incarnationally invitational is to commit to a shared life. It is a long-term investment in a relationship.

2. Being incarnationally invitational means caring more about being authentic than being comfortable. It's not invasive to invite someone to go somewhere with us. We are in control. Not only are we in control of the situation, but, more importantly, we are in control of how much we reveal of ourselves. When we limit ourselves to short spurts of time with people, we can play the game. We can fake it and only show them our best side.

Being incarnationally invitational is giving an invitation not to an event but into your life. If you truly invite people into your life, they see it all: the good, bad, and ugly. The rewards of open authenticity can have a profound impact on people.

3. Being incarnationally invitational means relationships flow out of real life. We've already exhausted the notions of how busy we all are. Being incarnationally invitational means investing in a relationship in the midst of the craziness. It's not a break in time; it is joint chaos. It is meeting people where they are in their current state of life, however calm or crazy that might be.

4. Being incarnationally invitational means life revolves more around people than events. Being incarnationally invitational is all about investing in people. It's more about inviting in than it is inviting out. What you actually "do" together is simply a product of the relationship and is inconsequential. The relationship trumps the events surrounding the relationship.

When the relationship trumps the events, you no longer judge an invite based on its level of excitement or "What's in it for me?" You simply invest because the relationship is important and is another opportunity for someone to see the power of Christ in your life.

Even though a concert might be more fun, the recital, graduation, or school play of a friend's child might be more important. It's the relationship that gets priority, not the circumstances around it.

5. Being incarnationally invitational means approaching relationships with purpose. An invite can be nothing more than some free time that you don't want to spend alone. It's uncommon to approach going to see a movie with someone as a part of some greater purpose.

However, to be incarnationally invitational is to develop relationships and invest time with purpose. It's not just a random string of invitations; every invite is an intentional decision to consciously carry the mission of Christ with you.

6. Being incarnationally invitational means saying yes. Scripture shows us the flip side of what it means to be incarnationally invitational, as well. The flip side is that someone who is incarnationally invitational does not always give the invitation; they are also someone who accepts the invitation. Jesus chose people. He wasn't saying yes to an endless string of "events." Jesus said yes to relationships. The situation didn't matter, the relationship did.

7. Being incarnationally invitational both expands and diminishes your network. Being incarnationally invitational expands your network because your life is an invitation. The invitation goes out to all regardless of similarities, differences, socioeconomic status, race, etc.

At the same time, your network becomes diminished because being incarnationally invitational means an investment in people within the constraints of time. To put it in other words, if you have $100, you could give 100 people $1, 10 people $10, or 1 person $100. The reality of being incarnationally invitational means you will give less people more time.

There are countless books about the ways Jesus approached relationships. He had a giant network of people in his life, and he was intentional with the time he gave to each group. Jesus' network could include the crowds, the followers, the apostles, the 70 he sent out, the 12 disciples, and the inner 3.

Jesus invested much more time in the inner three than he did the crowds. Likewise, being incarnationally invitational means investing fully in relationships, and it's impossible to invest fully in everyone.

What About Groups?

Most of what has been talked about in this section has been directed more toward personal expression—individuals embodying invitation as opposed to merely inviting. The idea being that by living out a life that is incarnationally invitational, we can be creating "groups" all the time. Creating a life lived in community, which should be the goal we aspire to as a body of Christians. It's a shift in thinking that sees all of life as potential group time.

However, this is not to say we can't incorporate this same shift into our existing groups. These four simple yet profound moves can help our groups embody invitation:

1. Move out of the living room. One small step for a group, one giant leap for Christ-centered community. Just. Get. Out. Of. The. Living Room. We all know we need to do it, but it's so hard to do!

I understand that we worked hard to get people out of the pews and into the living room. The benefits of that move have been tremendous, but there is another move to make. To live out an invitational life, you cannot close off any invitation possibility. Don't stop the movement of our churches by shutting up your group in a house indefinitely.

2. Move into relational "authentegrity." What we are proposing here can seem even more overwhelming and an addition to already busy life. Opening up your life so that it reflects an open invitation may appear to add more things to do. This is why the move has to be accompanied by "living real"—being invitational in activities that are already present in your life.

We have to be 100 percent authentic and operate with 100 percent integrity (authentegrity!). As we open up our lives, always making room for others to be alongside us and joining with others in what they are doing, we cannot afford to play the game or be dishonest. We cannot be upset when people say no, and we have to be honest in our own responses. If it is family night, then block it out. Put up the boundary and lovingly decline. If your neighbor has turned down your offer for a barbecue five times, move on to the next neighbor, but don't harbor ill feelings or hold a grudge.

One of the many remarkable parts of Jesus' life is that not everyone did follow him and not everyone asked him to recline at their table. Jesus didn't seem to lose any sleep over it; instead, his responses were always given with the utmost authentegrity. And it never slowed down his lifestyle of incarnational invitation.

3. Move to where people already are. Once you move out of the living room and have established relational authentegrity, move your group to where people are.

In the book *The Art of Neighboring*, by Jay Pathak and David Runyon, one of the authors tells a story of putting on this big Christian concert event. They invited everyone, expecting a few thousand people to show up. Only 200 actually did. At the same time just a block over, a local establishment had a concert going on with the exact crowd they had been expecting. That got the author thinking about what it would look like for those 200 people to be present for what was already going on in their community.[4]

In our city, a new initiative called *Voice* has recently been started. The idea is that the city listens to the voice of the community, represented by the individuals at the meeting, as they envision what Evansville will look like in the future. I went to the last meeting; there were 30 people in attendance. As I sat through the meeting, I couldn't help but think of the potential impact my group could have made by presenting (in familiar and relatable terms) the biblical worldview for Christ-centered community alive in the city. Then I began to think, what if all the groups in our church would have been there or, better yet, all the small groups from all the churches in Evansville!

Groups can make an untold difference by simply moving their group time, on occasion, to where people already are.

4. Move toward a multi-church (even city) model. There will always be a number of church denominations. I get that people need to express their praise in different ways, people respond better to different teaching styles, and all that.

But why does this segmenting off of the church have to extend to small groups?

A great point made in the book *To Transform a City*, by Eric Swanson and Sam Williams, is that we can make a greater impact on our cities through church unity. While we can't be unified in all doctrine and practices, unity can start around a unified purpose.

We need to open up an ecumenical network of Christians among our small group ministries to really make a move toward being incarnationally invitational within our cities. First off, it's just practical. We need to know what the churches in our community are doing and open up the possibility for Christians to collaborate in areas where they currently do not. If you have a dream for your neighborhood, wouldn't it be nice to know that someone on your block hosts a gathering of Christian brothers and sisters every week?

 This isn't about church growth; it is about kingdom growth. And it isn't about building a great church; it's about building a great city. Your small group can make the first move toward a multi-church model by inviting a group from another church to help with a service opportunity or raise funds together or any other of the limitless potential connection points. See where it goes and grows from there.

Chapter 13

PARADIGM SHIFT #3: FELLOWSHIP GROUPS TO MISSION TEAMS

BY AUSTIN

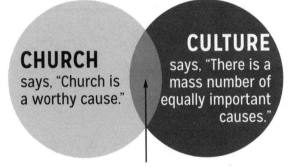

PROBLEM #3
People are passionate about doing something, yet there is a void of meaning in and for people's lives

CHURCH says, "Church is a worthy cause."

CULTURE says, "There is a mass number of equally important causes."

PARADIGM SHIFT #3
From fellowship groups to mission teams

Ghost Protocol

Thanks to the relatively recent release of *Ghost Protocol*, people of all ages have been exposed to *Mission Impossible*. To be honest, I think I only saw the first two, but what I remember about them was Tom Cruise, as Ethan Hunt, running around taking on the world pretty much by himself. Lots of action, lots of explosions, lots of death-defying completely unrealistic human activity—all for the greater purpose of truth, self-redemption, and national security. And, of course, the unforgettable line that seeped into our collective conscious: "Your mission, should you choose to accept it..."

Mission Impossible was originally a TV series that ran from 1966 to 1973 and was later revived from 1988 to 1990. The TV series wasn't so much about one guy as it was a team—the "Impossible Mission Force." The IMF agents were part-time operatives who held regular jobs in the real world of civilian activity. They were all ridiculously successful and rich, so not "real" in the terms of everyday life, but hey, it's TV. I'm surprised they had real jobs at all.

At the beginning of each episode, the Impossible Mission Force team leader would get a message from the "secretary" who would outline the mission. However, prefacing every message was the famous line, "Your mission, should you choose to accept it…" The reason for this line was made clear by the scope of the missions—they had been deemed impossible. They were outlandish and full of risk, with such high stakes you would have to be crazy to even entertain the possibility of accepting them. Enter the Impossible Mission Force.

This team of part-time espionage specialists, against all odds and in the face of sensible practicality and reason, never once declined a mission. Through two separate TV series, hundreds of episodes, and four movies, the IMF always accepted. Why? Because if they didn't, no one would. They were, after all, "impossible" missions. However, there was another reason just as important. The characters were made for it. They enjoyed it. It was their calling. It fulfilled their lives. When they were on a mission and accomplishing it, they were doing what they were put on the earth to do.

I loathe trite transition questions, but this is the appropriate place…

- Do we understand the impossible mission before us?

- Do we know how outlandish, risky, and high-staked the mission is?

- Do we see that if we don't answer the call, no one will?

- Do we truly understand that when we become justified through faith in Jesus Christ, we become God's Impossible Mission Force?

- Do we really believe that we now find our joy, calling, and fulfillment in life through participating in the mission of God?

- Do we realize we have already chosen to accept the mission?

God of Mission

Make no mistake, we serve a God of mission. The Bible continually paints the picture of a God who is on mission—One who acts, takes on the most impossible of all missions, and accomplishes it:

- Creating the cosmos—taking the void and meaningless, and infusing it with purpose and goodness

- Electing his people to bless the nations

- Rescuing them from slavery

- Fighting for them in battle

- Exiling them to cleanse and purify

- Returning them to their inheritance

- Giving hope through his Word

- Entering into his creation—becoming Incarnate

- Living a perfect life against all temptation

- Taking sin, taking death, defeating the enemy

- Conquering with grace and establishing eternal life

- Reigning over his eternal kingdom

- Consummating the victory

For some reason, God has allowed us to be in on the mission with him, the mission of rescuing his people and reconciling all things to himself. He uses people to reach people. God has gathered his IMF, and it's us—the church.

Returning to my trite questions…do we get this? More importantly, do we actually live it out? We are the front-line mission team sent in to achieve what the world has deemed impossible; armed with two weapons (love God, love your neighbor), we are to spread the kingdom of God that brings with it beauty, peace, love, purpose, meaning— in other words, the very presence of God—wherever the kingdom reigns.

That's what the Great Commission is all about. It is our mission directive. When Jesus said, "I will be with you always," he wasn't offering a feel-good statement. He was offering his life, which we as professing Christians have accepted. <u>We have received all power and authority in heaven and on earth. I fear we are wasting this power and authority by not using our groups and our churches as the Impossible Mission Force—people who know that their ultimate goal, their fulfillment of life, is to further the mission of God.</u>

To see this happen, we believe a paradigm shift needs to occur within our groups that moves them from fellowship groups to mission teams.

Mission-Minded Generation

I love what Craig Groeschel said to the emerging leaders at the 2012 Global Leadership Summit:

> *I believe in you…because you, the younger generation, are the most cause-driven, mission-minded generation in recent history. You care so much about those who are in need. And let me tell you—we weren't like that. We weren't like that. You don't want a job—you want a calling. You don't want to just make money—you want to make a difference. There is something inside of you that when you look at the injustices in this world you just say, "No! No! Not on my watch! I am not okay with that."[1]*

That is a serious compliment with serious implications. If Groeschel is right and this is the characteristic of the emerging generation, *they will do something.*

The next generation, or emerging generation, is often defined as 18 to 29 year olds. I happen to be just outside this age range, but as I look at my friends and acquaintances and look back at my own life, I see this sentiment alive everywhere. Even when I walked away from the church and was functionally agnostic, I still wanted to do *something*. So I signed up for the Peace Corps. Most of my friends within and without the Christian faith community want to do *something*. Lately, we've been slowed a bit by the "baby making" season of life, but my personal experience is right in line with Groeschel's assessment.

Putting that sentiment into practice is another story. There are a small group of leaders who are trying to make a difference, but the vast majority of the emerging generation, while ideologically holding to this sentiment, remain stuck when it comes to practically putting it into action.

I believe this is due to an underlying frustration that goes along with the drive to do something: They don't know what to do. Or they feel like they don't have an outlet to do anything substantively impactful.

There are (at least) three things that contribute to this underlying frustration:

1. Overwhelming Cacophony. With the flattening of the world has come the capability to see all the horror within it—and all the good—all at once. Famine, lack of water, genocide, human trafficking, cyclical poverty, addictions, tyranny—micro-lending, community development, TOMS shoes—starving children with no education, natural disaster relief. The circumstances of this world, coupled with the rise in numbers of people and organizations capable to combat it, can create a paralyzing apathy to the immensity of the noise it creates. There is so much to do and so much going on that it's hard to know what to do and how to devote your precious time and energy.

2. Sea of Skepticism. Remember our discussion about postmodernism in Paradigm Shift #1? Well the same cultural milieu that surrounded the authority of the Bible is still present, even when people are actively pursuing positive goals. Is that money really going to little kids? Does this truly matter? Who says this is the right thing to do? Bound to the emerging generation's will to act is a crippling skepticism that hinders action and slows progress. When you harbor disbelief toward narratives that remove the larger story of life, you lose the center that motivates action. You create a void of meaning and purpose that is tough to fill. The result is an emerging generation that wants to see change but does not trust existing institutions to enact that change. Some courageous, entrepreneurial spirits decide to start their own thing, but most of us simply don't know where to begin—and we aren't sure what we can or should do to make a difference.

3. Lack of Practical Outlet. So we have a whole generation of young adults who are amped up and ready to go. They want to make a difference. They want to change the world, and they will literally pour out their lives to meet the needs of others. Then they take a look around with all their pent up angst, energy, and good will and find nothing to connect it to. Every opportunity to make a difference either seems halfway across the world or sketchy or both. There doesn't seem to be anything tangible to grab hold of. Sure, you could dump some money, but this is a generation that needs to see the difference they are making—needs to feel a part of it. When they take a look at their immediate surroundings, they see no outlet for the difference they want to make. Whether out of a lack of effort or a lack of opportunity, the multitudes aren't connecting to action. Let's be honest, if the above descriptor by Groeschel of the emerging generation was being practically lived out by even 10 percent of them, this country, and probably the world, would begin to look completely different.

Richard Dawkins to the Pope

So far, most of this chapter has been directed toward and about the emerging generation, but in no way is it irrelevant to people all along the age spectrum. There are people who have grown metaphorically fat and lazy in their vision for their life. Plenty of people are blinded by a circumstance, business, or routine, which disallows them to think beyond their living space. However, most people want to know and believe that their life is making a difference.

From Richard Dawkins to the pope, we all want to make an impact and leave the world a better place despite our differences in how we might express our actions to achieve this goal. When I think of my parents, the 50-year-old single woman in our life group, the elders of our church, or my highly skeptical non-Christian neighbor, they all want to make a difference. It isn't an age thing so much as it is a life thing.

By extension, people want the actions they choose to contribute to this end. Individuals have to be intentional about what they decide to pour their lives into. Or at least they should! Earlier, Zach touched on the reality that when you say yes to one thing, you automatically say no to another. When I chose to play baseball in high school, I said no to track. When I chose to marry Chandra Lynn Jolliff, I said no to the Peace Corps. When I choose a Mister Misty Float, I say no to an Oreo Blizzard.

When we choose activities to add to our lives, we declare the meaning we have chosen to add to the world by sifting out what we say no to. What the church is asking people to choose (the activity we are asking them to add, causing them to say no to an infinite list of other potential possibilities) is small groups. And the predominant model right now within small group ministries across America is fellowship groups.

This reality is why we took such a long, extended look at small groups in the opening section, "Cultural Cows of Small Groups." Because it's time to be blunt. On one side of the cultural gap we have people looking for meaning. Not only meaning they can contribute to the world, but meaning they can add in their own lives. There's a seemingly endless flood of opportunity clamoring for the attention of people whose cause seems worthy and whose impact seems immense. On the other side of the gap is the church asking people to be involved in…fellowship groups?

Last chapter, in Paradigm Shift #2, we talked about how people are breaking down their lives into different tribes. You can be involved in exactly what you want with exactly who you want. And we, the church, tell relative strangers to group together arbitrarily for the sum total of fellowship. <u>We have an emerging generation who would die to make a difference. We have the most important mission in the history of the world given to us by a God of mission, who has given us all power and authority on earth through Jesus Christ to accomplish that mission. We even have a secret weapon at our disposal (the Holy Spirit) to aid us step-by-step in accomplishing the mission objectives. And we are asking people to fellowship?!</u>

The unfortunate truth of the cultural cows we explored is that we aren't even excelling in our pursuit of meaningful fellowship groups.

Mission Mentality

The paradigm shift we are proposing is to move away from small group ministries as fellowship groups and, rather, toward mission teams. Check out the advantages of shifting to a mission team mentality:

Missions are personal. "*Your* mission, should *you* choose to accept it…" There are no questions about who will own it, who will do it, who will take a step forward to relieve this holy discontent in the world. It's you! You step up. Seek what breaks God's heart, create a mission around it, and align it with what breaks your heart. Then get moving.

Missions are involved. Missions require research, strategy, and presence. There is no chance to "dump and run." A mission guarantees involvement because you can't rely on the experts and the people who are already doing it. You have to do it! So you'd better figure out how.

Missions generate excitement. "This message will self destruct in five seconds." And with that statement, the mission is underway—the clock is ticking. There is natural momentum and excitement that accompanies the acceptance of a mission.

Missions are creative. Think Tom Cruise dangling from thin wires. I don't remember a lot about the *Mission Impossible* movies, but that image of Hunt dangling from the wires is ingrained in pop culture. It's an image of creative problem solving. A mission requires you to think about accomplishing goals from a different angle or viewpoint.

Missions add value. "The fate of the world rests on your shoulders." Good small groups add value to the people in them. A mission not only adds value to the group, but it adds value into the lives of others being impacted by the mission. There are real problems in the world that affect real people. Having your group attack one of these problems will add real value.

Missions can be completed. "Mission accomplished." The amount of ills and needs in society can be overwhelming to the point of paralysis. If all these organizations and experts can't fix the problems, how can we? You can't! But it's possible to identify a part of the problem, create a mission around it, and set out to accomplish that mission. It may have a huge observable impact, or it might miss. Chances are it will land somewhere in between. But you can set a goal, evaluate your progress toward the end, and reach the finish. And possibly the greatest advantage is in the area of actual fellowship itself.

Missional Fellowship

Have you ever been on a mission with someone else or with a group of people? Maybe a short-term mission trip or a local project in your community that required leadership, vision, planning, organization, teamwork, and execution? What are the relationships like within that team? Especially if the scope of the mission seems larger than what you should be able to accomplish. Precisely because the mission is personal, involved, exciting, creative, and can be accomplished, the relationships end up being all the things small groups set out to be in the first place: natural, authentic, inviting, real, and personal.

An extreme analogy is a platoon or regiment in war. A bunch of people from all walks of life are thrown together. They are different ages, from different geographical locations, and have different personal hopes and aspirations. They are of different ethnicities and have different economic backgrounds, religious beliefs, and personalities. Yet they become a team, and through the intensity (and horrors) of combat, they even move beyond a team and become family. They end up forming a bond and a relationship that transcends anything that would have been possible without the unified vision of the mission. A group of people who may not have even liked one another otherwise experience true fellowship.

By getting groups on a mission, we will create more meaningful and natural fellowship, instead of trying to force fellowship in our weekly small group time.

When church is seen as just another social club, it's missing the mark on both fronts. It's leaving the greatest resource of the world untapped—the empowered church—and is failing to provide the dynamic witness that forces people to recognize the glory of God and makes outsiders want to get in on the movement.

Potential Energy

In the opening chapter, I talked about an experience with my friends where I realized we needed to open up different avenues for people to experience Jesus outside the Sunday morning worship time. As I saw that day through their eyes and experienced what was supposed to be God's redemptive plan of salvation and redemption for the world, I had to ask, "That's it?! That's what the church does?!" Let's flip their church experience. At the time of this writing, One Life Church has 65 groups. Imagine something with me:

- Imagine all of those groups digging around in God's Word to find where their passions in life and/or holy discontent intersects with the mission of God.

- Then, they explore the actual needs of the community around them. They find where those two things connect and frame a mission statement around it.

- Finally, they take their relatively puny vision for what they think they can accomplish and God-size it. Up the ante a bit and pray about that big audacious goal.

Imagine all 65 groups doing that. Would it not begin to change the culture of a community? Of a city even?

Now what if the vision becomes a movement and...

- The two megachurches in the city with their combined 400+ groups are doing the same thing.

- All the missional-minded church plants utilize their groups to the same end.

- All the older established churches combine their wisdom and resources.

- All the midsize family-oriented churches join in also.

And, well, you get the point. Imagine each and every one of those individual groups of Christians engaging the community with a specific mission. Not as some sort of "missional ideology," but as a real mission with a written-out mission statement, timeline, and measurable goal. Imagine those groups accomplishing their mission. Imagine the impact in the community and the city.

This isn't merely a pie in the sky dream; it is potential energy around a biblical promise. It is who we (the church) are called to be. We are the Impossible Mission Force for a God of mission.

Standing in a Gospel Movement

For the most part, we either aren't getting the memos, or unlike the *Mission Impossible* TV series, we are choosing not to accept the mission.

This is a sad state of affairs. There's an emerging generation, passionate about serving others, who can't settle for past generations' definition of success. They want a life filled with meaning and purpose, and they want to bring those same things into the lives of others. What they lack and need is an outlet.

The church has all these things in its arsenal. The meaning. The purpose. The application to life. As worshippers of the Creator of the cosmos, we know we can provide the foundation for serving that other worldviews ultimately cannot. Philippians 2:6-11 says:

> *Though he was God, he did not think of equality with God as something to cling to. Instead, he gave up his divine privileges; he took the humble position of a slave and was born as a human being. When he appeared in human form, he humbled himself in obedience to God and died a criminal's death on a cross. Therefore, God elevated him to the place of highest honor and gave him the name above all other names, that at the name of Jesus every knee should bow, in heaven and on earth and under the earth, and every tongue confess that Jesus Christ is Lord, to the glory of God the Father.*

Within those six brief verses alone, we have enough intellectual depth to rival any other system. We have a basis for life that supersedes the self, a more compelling story than has ever been told, and a limitless supply of motivational fuel to burn in order to sustain action—in order to see the good work of our Impossible Mission come to completion.

And I can't help but imagine one more thing: My friends standing inside a city in the middle of a Gospel movement. A movement where *real* needs are being met and the quality of life for real people is rising. A movement fueled by hundreds and hundreds of groups that are intentionally engaging people who are either far from God or far from the hope of God. All for the sake of the Gospel. I can imagine my friends sitting back and thinking, "This is it! I want to know a God who has *this* plan for people in the world!"

For a practical guide, resources for framing a group mission, and examples of what groups on mission could look like, go to culturalcows.com. We would love for you to share your experiences and success stories! Here are three examples of what groups on mission look like.

Group One

Bret and Stacey were part of a core team of a new church plant. After grouping with the pastor for a year leading up to the plant, they answered his invitation to lead a small group. They were naturally outgoing people, enjoyed building new relationships, and already saw themselves as "hosts." Small group leadership seemed like a perfect fit.

Their strengths came out right away as their group quickly grew and their living room filled up. Their love for people spilled out of them, and pretty soon their group was filled with Christ-centered fellowship. After some church connection events swelled their numbers even more, they were forced to close their group to new members because they just couldn't fit anyone else.

Bret and Stacey took their roles as small group leaders seriously. They loved the people in their group, worked hard to build actual relationships, and even developed real friendships with most of them. They even had the privilege of baptizing three group members!

After two years, though, something was missing. They did a service project every other month, but it seemed more like something they just did because they knew they were supposed to. They saw that the true strength of their group was in the relational fellowship that occurred during group time. They knew that people have a need for community, and they were meeting that need. They just felt like there was a lid on the impact they could be making.

Bret and Stacey asked the pastor for help getting over the hump, and he gave them resources, telling them to think and pray about multiplication. After reading the books, they saw that their passion for fellowship and Christ-centered community could be cross-positioned with multiplication. They decided to build on their strengths and get on a mission.

They started by introducing the idea of multiplication to their group. Many of the people, especially their closest friends, were skeptical. But the enthusiasm and excitement of a fearless leader is contagious, and they decided to hold a group brainstorming session on how to make this happen in their group.

Through much deliberation, and some gnashing of teeth, the group settled on this mission statement: We will multiply our group from one to two healthy groups within 6 months.

Bret (ever the adventurous one) reminded the group of a book they had read a few months earlier called *Sun Stand Still*. He said, "Let's take this vision beyond our comfort zones!"—so they changed their mission to multiplying groups that would in turn multiply themselves within 12 to 18 months. Within 5 to 7 years, the goal changed from aiming for one group of 20 people to 16 groups of 300 people. They diagrammed it with measurable goals like this:

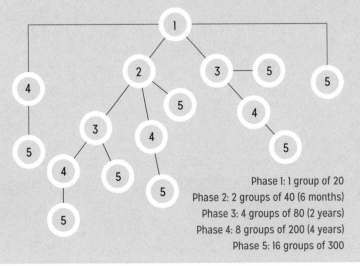

Phase 1: 1 group of 20
Phase 2: 2 groups of 40 (6 months)
Phase 3: 4 groups of 80 (2 years)
Phase 4: 8 groups of 200 (4 years)
Phase 5: 16 groups of 300

They then constructed a plan to make that vision a reality. They knew they needed two things—16 leaders and 300 people!

Leaders: They wanted to launch healthy groups, so they immediately identified not one but three potential leaders. That way each group would have two leaders even after launching. To help model multiplication, they incorporated breakouts into every group time. Each leader would take smaller groups of 4 to 5 people each week for a set amount of time to practice facilitating discussion and organizing group time.

300 people: Even though their group was "full" now, they knew that if they were going to reach 300 people, they would have to make bringing in new people a part of their group DNA. So they came up with three ideas that would help:

1. Lobby missionaries. They decided to be a group that treated Sunday mornings as a time to engage people in the lobby, having conversations about groups. They made it a "requirement" for everyone in the group to introduce themselves to someone, get their name, and ask them at some point in the conversation, "Whose group are you in?" If they weren't in one, they got an invite. If they were, they talked about their respective groups. They built a report back/story sharing time into their weekly group meetings.

2. Not only who, but how. This was Bret and Stacey's version of the empty chair. Every week they would have a few people from the group share someone from their life who might be a good person to bring to group. They named names of real people. But they didn't stop there. They would talk about how they might get them to come, and they would actually do it. Sometimes it was as easy as an invitation; sometimes it meant going bowling or grilling out.

3. Block parties. They planned block parties for each other and organized one before every launch of a new group. Who better to begin building relationships with than their actual neighbors?

Bret and Stacey's group is just underway in this vision. They've launched their first group (phase two), and it has added tremendous value to their group. It has brought revitalized energy and a new sense of purpose and meaning. They have added a Facebook group page and a biannual reunion gathering to the original plan, so they can see and track kingdom growth and celebrate their mission as they go. Getting their group on a mission did not detract from the strengths of their group, it actually helped heighten their giftings of fellowship and relationship building, and it brought focus to what they were already passionate about.

Group Two

This group formed nearly 20 years ago. They have literally grown old together. They have moved from a group of 8 to 12 couples with a cackle of kids to a group of empty nesters.

They bought in completely to the discipleship small group model and saw group time as a time when they could deepen their relationship with Jesus.

Over the years they have dug into many studies and have truly grown together spiritually and as friends.

About a year and a half ago, a new pastor came in and started to talk a lot about breaking out of the Christian huddle. He even introduced a revised mission of the church, changing it to "Helping people far from God experience Jesus." A new wave of younger adults now come to church, which has energized and excited this group, but they aren't exactly sure how and where they fit in.

After taking a class called "Live Your Mission," this group decided to accept a challenge and explore how their group might further the mission of the church in its own unique way.

They ended up deciding together to study 1 Timothy. But instead of the normal approach, they were going to use the trust they had built up over the years to really wrestle through questions about what they were studying. They went all the way back to questions they hadn't thought about in years like, "Why should we accept the Bible as the authoritative Word of God in the first place?" and "Who is Timothy?"

And instead of asking, "What does this passage mean to us?" they decided to ask, "What would this passage mean to someone who doesn't fully believe in God and Jesus and how might we clearly explain the truths of Scripture to that person?"

They decided to use the fall season to create and write a study designed specifically for a non-Christian to go through 1 Timothy and explore the issues of faith within it. Their group mission statement was this: As a group, create a 6-week study on 1 Timothy, specifically for people exploring faith.

After creating the study, they showed it to the pastor. He put it out in the church's resource center, and the small groups pastor ended up using it in a combined curriculum campaign. The group is looking to see if they can get it published to reach a wider audience, and they are already looking forward to framing their next mission.

Group Three

Two couples from church have kids on the same baseball team. They sit next to each other at every game and talk about how they would love to join a small group, but they're just too busy with all the kids' activities. Besides, they serve on a kids' ministry team on Sunday mornings. Eventually they will join a group, once life slows down a bit.

One day they were challenged by a teaching on living missionally and decided they could apply it to the baseball team. They came up with a prayer that became a mission statement: "Lord, help us to be the body of Christ among the parents and families on this baseball team. Help us to love them and to build relationships that will hopefully open up opportunities for us to share the good news of Jesus with them."

They divided up the names of the boys on the team and committed to pray for each of them on their morning drives to work.

One couple invited the team and parents over to their house to make team shirts. They organized a baked goods sale with other parents from the team and used the funds to buy appreciation gifts for the coaches. To their surprise, at the end of the season several parents approached them and asked what the plans were for the year-end party.

Group Four

John had never been to church, but upon hearing about a new church that started in his neighborhood, he went on launch day. He fell deeply in love with Jesus and eventually began feeling called to lead.

There was just one big problem: He didn't know where he fit into "church" leadership. He was not a kids guy, and no one had ever accused him of being a people person. He certainly didn't feel like he had enough answers for questions people might have about faith.

He also had a pretty rough past. He had never felt judged by the church—actually he felt just the opposite—but was convinced that if he tried to lead anything, the other shoe would drop.

Then John heard about some grants the church was giving out to help get some community development underway in the neighborhood. On a whim, he applied for $1,000 to buy an old clunker and some parts, so he could fix the car up and give it to a single mother who lived a few doors down from him. He literally could not believe it when he was informed he would receive the grant money! He called back three times to make sure he had heard right.

He was so excited he just couldn't quit talking to people about it. Pretty soon, he had a couple guys from church, a co-worker, and two of his buddies from his party days coming over most Friday nights to work on the car together.

John often found himself simply telling stories about how Jesus had changed his life and about the things he was reading in the Bible and praying to God about. These things would just pop up in the normal flow of conversation while working on the car.

It took about 7 months to finish the project, but not one of those men ever forgot the feeling of delivering the car to that single mother.

The next Friday, John got a call from one of his unchurched friends who had helped out. He said, "I know this other lady in my neighborhood who could really use a car..."

After that conversation, John decided he would keep the Friday night thing going. He wasn't sure how he was going to get the money for the next clunker and parts or if all the guys would keep coming back, but it didn't matter. He blowtorched a message on his wall that said, "In this garage, we build because we are rebuilt."

Beauty of Mission

The beauty of groups getting on a mission is that you don't have to adopt any sort of small group model or pigeonhole Christian community. The above examples span everywhere from the typical small group models to small groups that could never be tracked and/or recognized by a "church metric."

The common unifier among these four stories is that the people accepted a call to impact their communities. They got on a mission to bring the body of Christ, the Light of the world, into the lives of people around them.

Part Three:
THE BIG FINISH

Chapter 14

BLOW IT UP

BY ZACH

Erasing History

Here's the big question: What if small groups never existed? What if the '80s megachurch explosion was erased from our history and groups had never been formed?

Today's trends show that we're faced with the problem of massive amounts of people abandoning ship. We look around and see our communities full of need. We see massive groups of people, including friends and family, saying that living life unexamined, apathetic, or as a nonpracticing Christian makes more sense than having a relationship with God.

We see Christians huddled up in churches, over-programmed and unavailable to the community, all the while desperately wanting to make a difference…an impact. We want our friends, family, and co-workers who are far from God to know the transforming power of Jesus. But they need more than a church service or church group.

At the same time, we desire deeper, more meaningful relationships as well. We want to see how other Christians go through life, actively living out faith alongside them. We want to grow closer to God through relationships. How do we do it?

We hold meetings, we analyze data, and someone says, "We've got to get out of the building and break down into smaller Christian communities."

Everyone agrees, and someone else says, "Great idea. Now how do we do it? What do these groups or 'communities' look like? What is their purpose? Goal?"

Evolve or Die

There is a saying in business: "Evolve or die." It's a simple sentiment with an obvious connotation—culture, the market, and communication methods change. Even the way people approach life as a whole is in a constant state of flux. Businesses cannot simply bury their heads, ignoring the movement, and expect to remain relevant. There are countless stories of major companies that have ignored the cultural and philosophical changes being made in the world and paid the price for it.

Atari: Atari was *the* video gaming system in the '70s and early '80s. They had the market share and could direct the future of video games. Along came a new company called Nintendo, offering to let their products be licensed and sold under the name Atari. Atari couldn't come to an agreement, and we know what happened. More than 20 years later, Nintendo is still relevant and Atari is nothing more than an antiquated piece of history. Atari was making it. What they were doing was working. Then all of the sudden, it stopped working, and it was too late.

AOL: If you were around when AOL broke into the mainstream, then you'll probably never forget the sound of your computer dialing—the buzzes and beeps while establishing connection—and the magic words "You've got mail." Founded in the '80s, America Online established itself as the online service for computer newbies. They had a software suite that provided a simple and straightforward method for using the Internet. However, over the years the average Internet user evolved and AOL did not. Even after a merger with Time Warner, AOL could never reclaim its spot at the top of the Internet food chain. They failed to evolve alongside the average user's technical abilities, and they paid the price for it.

Kodak: Kodak is the newest to the news of historic companies filing for bankruptcy protection. What most people don't know is that Kodak actually invented the first digital camera in the 1970s but didn't release the technology for fear that it would eat up their profits in the film and film development market. They tried to hang on to film as long as they could. Then, digital cameras hit the mass market, and new names began to emerge in the photography industry. They could've paved the way for culture but chose to rest on the hope that what worked well early would always work well.

Yes, Another Facebook Study

There are major success stories of businesses that have kept a watchful eye on culture and never settled for anything less than greatness—companies that had a great product but evolved to make an even better product that would change the way society functions.

You can't look at successful and innovative companies and not talk about Facebook. Think and say what you want about it, but you cannot deny that the company has had enormous influence on culture today. However, when you look back over Facebook's short history, you can see a few key evolutionary decisions that made the difference between "just another tech company" and being catapulted into history.

In 2004, Facebook, or "Thefacebook" as it was first called, was created. Initially Thefacebook was open only to Harvard students. Following initial success, Thefacebook extended membership to students at Stanford, Columbia, and Yale and then on to all Ivy League schools. The company dropped the "the" from its name, settling on the name Facebook. It didn't take long for Facebook to open up to all universities, then high school students, and finally anyone over the age of 13 with a valid email address.

I remember hearing the chatter about Facebook. I was still hanging out over in the world of MySpace, and all of the college students at the church I was working at were telling me, "Man, you gotta switch to Facebook." The only problem was that I couldn't—I wasn't a college student. To be a member of Facebook at that time, you had to have a valid college or high school email address. Facebook was already available to thousands of colleges and high schools throughout the world. Even the greatest critics would say that at the time Facebook was already a *giant* success. They had the college market nailed!

What if Facebook stopped there? What if they settled for being a place college kids could gather online? Would they have still been successful? Probably. Would they have steered culture? Probably not.

Facebook had a choice: stay in its current form and enjoy success among college students, or take a chance and seek out something truly special. One billion Facebook users later, and we know what was chosen.

<u>Companies that don't examine themselves through the filter of a changing culture are forced to suffer the consequences.</u>

Evolution of Groups

Throughout the entirety of this book, we have consistently revisited a claim that really is self-evident through simple observation. A claim that is obvious to all who look around—culture is vastly different than it was 30 years ago.

In contrast, our groups have spent the last 30 years huddled in living rooms as the world outside continues to change. To steal Austin's analogy, we are sitting around a boom box jamming out to a cassette of '80s Christian music while the rest of the world has moved on.

Full Circle

So here we are, full circle. The reality is that small groups do exist. We can't go back 30 years and erase their history, nor should we.

Let me ask a real question that is meant to be genuinely wrestled with—not just taken hypothetically.

What if we blew up our groups?

What if this Sunday from the pulpit your small groups pastor said, "We are closing the book on small groups. Each group must dissolve, effective immediately"? What would happen?

- The first question to ask: Would Christian community cease to exist?

- The follow-up question: Would groups begin to form naturally within this community?

- And finally: What would they look like and what would their purpose be?

Somewhere in the answers to these questions there is a secret to the potential of Christian community. We challenge you to break out the whiteboard and ask these questions. Let's start with a new canvas instead of trying to paint within the picture that already exists. The truth is, we are limiting our leaders, and therefore our groups, by trapping them inside any small group model.

Transitioning Groups

To achieve the suggested shifts, groups must start informally and empower people with the freedom to express Christian community in wildly original and creative ways. Being a trendy church of small groups must take a backseat to being a church devoted to reaching unchurched, secular-minded people. Reaching these people can happen through groups of Christians who live out their faith in ways that are truly on mission. Groups that naturally create disciples—holding one another accountable to living lives of worship. Groups that are authentic, biblical, and live life together in a very real way—all while having the freedom to do so in whatever way is best for a group to achieve that end. These groups are the way to reach people, no matter what they look like and no matter how hard they may be to measure.

Austin and I are in the process of doing this. We have a detonator in one hand and a dry erase marker in the other. We have introduced these shifts to the groups and leaders at our church and are in the process of forming a safe structure for willing groups to make this transition. We are identifying "pilot groups" who want to take these broad principles, focus them, and turn them into a practical reality. More than anything, we are looking for people who see groups as the number one untapped resource for impacting the lives of people around us. People who see a group of Christians as raw material to mine, draw out of their slumber, and shape into a tool for community-transforming and world-changing impact.

Follow along and see what happens at culturalcows.com.

Chapter 15

THE LAST CULTURAL COW: UNTAPPED POTENTIAL

BY AUSTIN

Chasing vs. Creating Culture

I vividly remember in seminary when a flip switched inside me and the Gospel of Jesus Christ, the metanarrative of Scripture, became a way of living instead of a theoretical academic pursuit. It was a very naive and ideologically driven birthplace. I remember the roller coaster waves of emotion after truly believing in God's love for us as expressed through his Son and sustained through his Spirit. That out of his infinite love, compassion, and beauty, he allows us in on his mission to save the world.

I first looked around frantically, wanting to get in on this revolution that certainly was about to rock the world. I didn't want to miss out! Then I looked around in confusion as the life-changing, world-altering message of the good news hardly seemed to make a difference in the lives of people professing to be followers of Christ. Finally, I remember weeping (metaphorically) in frustration over the Light of the world being covered and having a panicky feeling about what to do to remedy the situation.

After taking a chill-pill, I realized I just had to do *something*. I needed to take a small step forward in faith into my sphere of influence and see what happens. What my family and I decided to do was start a house church network called Lampstand Ministries, which God saw fit to use to completely reshape me and take me, personally, very far outside my comfort zone. More on that to come.

The franticness, frustration, and panicky feelings that would periodically resurface used to freak me out—until I heard Bill Hybels' talk on "Holy Discontent." These feelings would always resurface surrounding the tension between what I find in God's Word and what I find in the world. It always led me back to the questions: "Why? Why does it have to be this way? Why does the church always have to chase culture?"

Historical Revolution

Historically the church has *not* always chased culture. If every person in the world was in the same book club and by a miracle of random selection I had the first choice of which book to read, I would choose *Atheist Delusions* by David Bentley Hart. Although I suppose I would let them substitute *Who Is This Man?: The Unpredictable Impact of the Inescapable Jesus* by John Ortberg (an easier to read, more motivational book that covers the same general points and is equally impactful). Both books give a detailed, historical account of how the church has not always been simply chasing culture. There was a time when the church actually created culture.

There was a time when the church...

- Changed the view and role of women in society

- Questioned and eventually abolished slavery

- Broke down class barriers that were responsible for centuries of generational poverty

- Brought health and purity to marriage and sexual relationships

- Advanced scientific discoveries at unprecedented rates

- Inspired artists to new heights

- Spurred on the greatest thinkers and philosophers

- Led to the construction of centers of learning that educated the masses

- Galvanized business and commerce

- Revolutionized healthcare

- Epitomized human rights

There will always be a need to fill the gap between church and culture, because there will always be a new generation emerging that needs to hear the good news in a different way. Every new generation brings subtle shifts, and occasionally these subtle shifts combine with innovations (Internet, civil rights, industry, etc.) to create seismic shifts that make the established way of things seem archaic. Progress is inevitable.

As good as we feel our proposed shifts are, in 30 years these conversations will be dated. That is a guarantee. Whenever truths are outwardly expressed, the expression itself has a shelf life no matter how timeless the truths. There will always be a need to recast the vision due to the inaction surrounding the vision. Have you ever read the Didache? Come on!

> If you're scratching your head at the Didache line, you're not alone. I have no idea what Austin is talking about, but for some reason he finds it hilarious. I find the fact that he actually believe it's funny to be hilarious. Austin's told me you can find out more about this fascinating ancient document at earlychristianwritings.com.

There will always be people who reject the message or close their ears to it who need to hear it afresh in new and creative ways. I understand the practical side. Yet something still whispers to me, "Why?" The church has done it before; can it not do it again? Can the church not be such a force that its detractors bemoan the overwhelming good it is producing, rather than say, "That's it?! This is what the church does?!"

Roman Emperor Julian the Apostate, who is most known for wishing to return the Roman Empire to paganism, wrote a letter in frustration over the fact that his pagan priests were not keeping up with the Christians in the empire:

> *I think that when the poor happened to be neglected and overlooked by the priests, the impious Galileans observed this and devoted themselves to benevolence...The*

impious Galileans support not only their poor, but ours as well, everyone can see that our people lack aid from us.[1]

The impact the Christian church had on culture and the lives of individuals was so undeniable that even the man whose nickname was "Apostate" (in this context meaning someone who forsakes Christianity) had to recognize the positive force of the "Galileans." Christians were not sucking the value out of culture—they were adding infinite value to it.

Integrated Church

How can this come about again? In our American culture, the vast majority of non-Christians say Christians are hypocritical, anti-homosexual, judgmental, too political, and sheltered.[2] And young adults are fleeing churches by the droves, because they see them as overprotective, shallow, anti-science, repressive, exclusive, and doubtless.[3] So how can the church again be described as "enjoying the goodwill of all the people. And each day the Lord added to their fellowship those who were being saved" (Acts 2:47). How can it again be said that the church is revolutionizing our view of the world?

Imagine each entity that makes up society (business, government, arts and entertainment) as its own silo—all working within close proximity to each other and yet separated by their ideologies and functionality. When the church shifts from acting as a separate silo to again becoming an integrated part of every aspect of society, it can transform cities, create a new culture, and change the world.

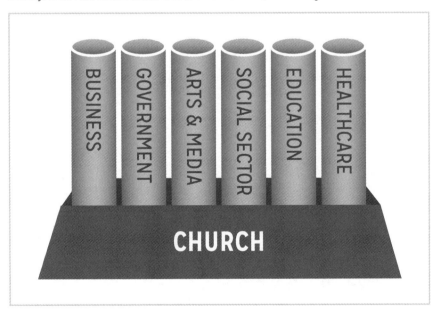

Before people integrate church into everything they do, they have to integrate Christ into who they are. And that will not come about on a large scale until, as I've heard Erwin McManus put it, the church reclaims its rightful place as the epicenter of human creativity.

Freedom to Create

Typically when people use the word "creativity" they jump to the arts, which is well and good and true. But what we are talking about here is the more general act of creating. It's the ability to transcend normal ideas, rules, patterns, and relationships and infuse them with life.

In this sense, God did two marvelous acts of creating:

1. Taking nothing and creating something.

2. Creating the means through which we, while being *somethings*, can tap into that something and create out of it ourselves.

That is the great story we have to tell. It's all in there—creation, covenant, exile, return, Christ, consummation—all of it tells the Love Story of a God who created and allows us to create. This is the ultimate freedom, the ultimate expression of life. Yet, too often, we are guilty of closing off creation. The church should be the heartbeat that pumps creativity through the veins of the world.

If the church was creating in ways that tapped into the story of the Creator in all the areas represented in the above illustration, then culture would be more than impacted—worldviews would begin to change, and the cultures of our cities would transform.

People like Eric Swanson, Sam Williams, Erwin McManus, and Tim Keller have spoken on this subject in much more comprehensive and eloquent ways, but we want to look briefly at how groups in particular are perfectly situated to contribute to this movement and are actually vital to it.

If our groups are creatively communicating the Gospel—while living out life in real ways, acting on a specific mission, being incarnationally invitational as they go—they can do more than merely close the gap between church and culture. They can also create culture through:

1. Collective Action

2. Collective Influence

3. Collective Impact

4. Collective Creativity

5. Collective Optimism

Collective Action

It may have seemed earlier that we beat up on accountability a bit. We were merely questioning whether the current understanding of accountability in small groups is fruitful. We believe groups should specifically be used to help spur each other on toward personal daily prayer and reflection on Scripture. Accountability absolutely should have a place in our groups. But instead of a weird and awkward confession time with people we are still developing trust and relationships with, we need to be holding one another accountable to living lives of worship. This should be our inspiration and driving force in spreading the kingdom of God here on earth. It should call us into action—not out of obligation, but out of joy in realizing the overflowing abundance of goodness available to us through the gift of Jesus Christ.

The hardest step in accomplishing something is doing anything; this is the power of living in Christian community. When it's functioning properly, we not only have the basis for action, but we have the support structure for sustainable action. As I write this, I know that tonight I'm going to wrap presents at Barnes & Nobles for an AIDS fundraiser. I know that 6 to 10 brothers and sisters in Christ will accompany me. I also know that my default mode, and probably that of most of the others in our group, is to go home after work and enjoy a nice relaxing night of dinner, family, and some form of passive entertainment. Not bad things in and of themselves. Important things really, but they miss the mark if they are the sum total of our activity. Tonight we will overcome our default modes in order to be present in our community as the body of Christ, because we are accountable to each other to live lives of worship.

When we talk about changing and creating culture, the first step is to simply be active in the world. Small groups allow us to participate in this activity in community and in ways that create an impetus for change.

Collective Influence

Picture this scene: A lone figure standing in the middle of a field during the first snowfall of the year. With arms outstretched, she spins around in circles, looking up into the sky with a smile on her face as snowflakes fall gently onto her skin. Then, *bam!* She gets smoked upside the head with a well-packed snowball. What got her attention? Which one made the greater impact?

Okay, so it's not a perfect metaphor. But our individual lives being lived out in pursuit of the love of Christ at work, play, and in our interactions with others is the foundation and beauty that can potentially blanket our world. Occasionally, though, you have to pull those snowflakes together in order to pack a wallop.

We absolutely have to saturate our world with individual faith in action if we are going to create culture, but a few strategically aimed snowballs of Christian community are needed for larger impact.

Groups tend to draw eyes and garner the attention that individuals simply don't or can't. We are fooled by our individualistic and personality-driven society into believing that we don't need others to accomplish what needs to get done. The truth for most of us is that on a day-to-day, real-life basis, we only carry enough influence and attention to land and make that brief tingly feeling that eventually melts into nothing. On the other hand, a group of people, particularly a Christ-centered group of people, have the potential to pool their expertise and collective relational capital in order to make people take notice.

Collective Impact

For children of the '80s, *Voltron* is an animation classic. The red, yellow, green, blue, and black lions were awesome fighting machines alone, but when they came together they formed Voltron—a giant super robot that defended the galaxy from evil. Separately they could fight, but together they were unstoppable.

Similarly, when different groups of unique people come together, they maximize their potential. Of course this would require us doing one of two things in the formation of our groups:

1. Thoroughly mine the passions, skills, and interests of the randomly put together people within our groups and tailor our actions to meet those characteristics.

2. Be intentional on the front end, grouping people together who compliment each other for maximum impact.

Either way would be suitable. Both would require focus, intentionality, and resources of the church. With as much time and resources as we spend on programming and group curriculums, could we not redirect efforts to try something new? Can we afford not to?

After Jesus ascended to heaven, the body of Christ coming together for unity was not only so the church could be healthy and successful in its pursuits—it was also to maximize its potential.

Jesus said, "I am in them and you are in me. May they experience such perfect unity that the world will know that you sent me and that you love them as much as you love me" (John 17:23).

Paul said, "He makes the whole body fit together perfectly. As each part does its own special work, it helps the other parts grow, so that the whole body is healthy and growing and full of love (Ephesians 4:16).

As groups come together, the people transform into something they could not be on their own. The church swells, and the world knows.

Collective Creativity

As the people in my small group know, I'm a brainstorming fanatic. Possibly to a fault. I frequently hold brainstorming group times and call "timeout" to what we are doing in order to dream up new ideas.

People are inherently creative. Unfortunately, most of the time our creative thinking remains locked inside our own minds. Brainstorming allows us to speak aloud those crazy ideas we have dreamt up. And do you know what happens when you speak them out loud with a group of people? They lose some of their craziness. Because Jim knows a guy who does something like that, and Tracy has written a grant for a playground before, and Bob works in the city zoning office—the ideas that seemed impossible begin to find a glimmer at the end of the tunnel. Then someone comes up with a completely new way of approaching another thought, and someone else adjusts it here, tweaks it there—and the impossibility of a good idea that was trapped inside of an individual now has probability behind it that was advanced by the group.

There is a reason universities and governments use "think tanks" to create—because they work. Our neighborhoods and communities need the people within them to tap into creative solutions.

Collective Optimism

Nothing changes culture for the good more effectively than positivity. The opposite is devastatingly true as well: Nothing wrecks culture more quickly than negativity. One person alone, having a positive attitude about their community, can be easily passed off as the well-meaning, naïve person who drew smiley face sunshines all over everything when they were a kid. This may seem obviously simplistic. But when 8, 12, or 20 people come with a positive attitude, positively go about their work, and positively create change, it begins to transform the overall outlook of the community. And over the long term it can even create a new culture within it.

Many factors go into creating the wider culture. Decades of deceased philosophers have more influence than most people know. Trends in science and economics, the media, political leaders, and influential people all contribute and interweave to create culture; but the masses determine what is ultimately accepted and what stays en vogue. When you move down to the micro level, where you have pockets of subcultures that our groups can actually influence, something as simple as positivity can (and will, in my opinion) create a new day—one where anything can seem achievable.

The Story of Lampstand Ministries

In 2010, we started planting a church called Lampstand Ministries. You won't find it on a Google search, and it will never get mass recognition or fame. From start to finish it only lasted 14 months. By many standards, it was unsuccessful and a failure. Yet, I want to briefly share our story here because it highlights the two greatest secrets of small groups.

The whole organic/missional community and house church movement is very trendy. It is kind of the yin to the contemporary megachurch movement's yang. However, we didn't know this at the time we were searching through ministry possibilities after seminary. God just kept putting the faces of my friends (like my golfing buddies) in my mind's eye over and over again. To use the phrase I both love and hate…"we felt called" to do ministry in my hometown of Evansville, Indiana where many of those faces resided. We looked around at all the great churches and the overwhelming volume of traditional churches in the community and decided a house church network was more in line with our particular bent and the niche available to us within the city.

We had absolutely no clue what we were doing. None. I had never worked for a church nor had I been in formal leadership capacity at any level. We had no money, no experience, and no established model to work from. All we knew was that God's Word tells us we are the light of the world, not to be hidden. And for some of our closest friends, that light had been snuffed out all together. Our mission was to create comfortable environments for people to explore God and experience Jesus. By doing this, we felt we were bearing the light of Christ into the world—hence the name "Lampstand."

We started small, inviting 26 adults to a 7-week vision-casting and explanatory orientation of our overall plan. Coming straight out of seminary, I remember that the original plan was to start with an 8-week class on church doctrine and history—before even explaining to these people what they were doing there in the first place! Hah!

Out of those 26 adults, 22 of them became our core team. We officially launched two house churches coming out of our first praise gathering on 10/10/10. Hindsight being so keen, we should have kept that core group together as one house church for a longer period, but we were just so stinking excited about the power of multiplication. We were going to plant Lampstands all throughout the city. We had this beautiful vision of a darkened city map, and as we launched each house church, we saw another light being turned on, and another, and another, until our entire city was flooded with the light of Christ being lived out in Christian community.

We poured the DNA of multiplication into our core team. We told them time and again that they were leaders, that they were expected to lead, and that they would one day lead a house church of their own. The books *Viral Churches* by Ed Stetzer and Warren Bird, *Exponential* by Dave Ferguson and Jon Ferguson, and *Total Church* by Tim Chester and Steve Timmis in a way became our handbooks. We believed Jesus when he said the kingdom of God has been established through him, and we were eager to see that kingdom explode in the city of Evansville.

There is much more to this story that can't be told here. The quick version is that after 9 months, vision had leaked, I was completely and totally burned out, we quickly scaled our house church network of two back down to one, and we were questioning the long-term sustainability of what we were doing.

It was precisely at this point when God intervened in each of those areas. God, I will never understand why you take us through the desert, but I am eternally grateful that you are present there and gracious enough to still lead us through to the Promised Land despite our grumblings.

When Lampstand Ministries was at its lowest point, God began to further his vision. He began bringing us relationships that built me up and encouraged me as a leader. He used a stranger to financially stabilize our home, which had been a constant source of draining doubt and anxiety. This reinvigorated me personally and solidified my resolve to lead in the direction that God had been pulling us toward. We came up with a plan to trim away the fat from our activities and focus on the mission, the original intent of why we started something in the first place. We came up with a new strategy for *healthy* multiplication. More than anything, we simply recaptured the excitement of a close relationship with Jesus and the endless potential that flows out of that.

Just about the exact time we were all jazzed up about our new direction and set to do the hard work of turning vision into reality, God showed us an even greater potential. A God-sized and God-directed vision.

Through the relationships mentioned earlier, we became connected with One Life Church, a church plant that had also launched on 10/10/10, with a slightly more voluminous effect. Their aim was to be a church planting network, and their second plant was set to be on the westside of Evansville, where we happened to be focusing our attention. The guy, Trey, who ended up being identified as the campus-pastor-to-be, had been mentoring me through the church planting process. Trey had also become a close friend.

After seeing lead pastor Bret Nicholson's heart for reaching unchurched, secular-minded people and hearing the mission of helping people far from God experience Jesus, I was hooked. I immediately went back to Trey and said, "How can we partner with you on a deeper level?" To which he replied, "Why don't you just stop what you're doing, join up with us, and help launch the One Life West campus." It was a little more than I had in mind, but after some formalities and a brief transition period of wrapping up our stuff, that is exactly what we did.

In doing so, the oversight, leadership, and resources available through the One Life network immediately answered the question of long-term sustainability. All three problems had now turned into answered prayers, and what God has done and continues to do through that has been incredible.

Out of the 22 people who made up our core team of Lampstand, 16 are now currently leading a life group through One Life. After 11 months of pouring into people with seemingly no traction, once we aligned the vision of our ministry with what God was doing, it simply exploded. In a year and a half, we went from one house church with about 30 people involved to eight small groups helping about 120 people live in Christian community. What's more, we are already seeing the third generation, as these groups are launching new groups. All of these groups have the DNA of multiplication and are being missional in the communities they live in. They have retained the vision of being the church and living out their faith outside the Sunday morning worship experience.

The vision has not stopped there. One Life Church now has 65 groups with more than 800 people living in Christian community. The vision for Gospel lights springing up all over our city has grown exponentially faster and has created a bigger impact than what we ever could have hoped or imagined as Lampstand Ministries.

Capitalizing on Potential

As wild and exciting as this journey has been, it's just a story of one church. The number of people and groups might be inspiring to some churches, and it might be small potatoes for others. What it has really served to do is broaden our perspective for the larger Christian community to see its potential.

Thinking about the collection of small groups present among all the churches throughout our own city and throughout the nation and the world, there is a seedbed for seeing Gospel city movements come to fruition—with groups being a vehicle for making it happen. There are groups everywhere! These lights are present in neighborhoods and communities all over. All we need to do is activate them and get their lights to turn on.

Jesus Christ was and is the fulfillment of life. This is the truth that the church has been sent into the world to share and live out. It's heartbreaking to see the church as anything other than that. It strips the Gospel of its power when our actions reflect anything else.

Smaller groups of Christian communities can help the church reclaim its rightful spot as the epicenter of human creativity—to be the liberators of humanity. Our job is to call people out of their ordinary lives and into their created intent of extraordinary relationship with their Creator.

Groups are already in place and ready to rock. We believe they just need a little tweak in what they do and produce. The three shifts we proposed are really meant to work together as our groups get on a specific mission in the community, creatively communicate the Gospel into the context of that mission, and become incarnationally invitational as the body of Christ. The image of the world dwelling in the presence of God can break through the lives of people who do not yet know God. We have access to the greatest gift imaginable:

> That is why they stand in front of God's throne and serve him day and night in his Temple. And he who sits on the throne will give them shelter. They will never again be hungry or thirsty; they will never be scorched by the heat of the sun. For the Lamb on the throne will be their Shepherd. He will lead them to springs of life-giving water. And God will wipe every tear from their eyes. (Revelation 7:15-17)

If we can activate our groups, we are perfectly positioned to usher in a fresh explosion of compassion. By doing so, God's name will be made famous, and he will make his glory known through the spreading of his kingdom:

> When I turned to see who was speaking to me, I saw seven gold lampstands. And standing in the middle of the lampstands was someone like the Son of Man. He was wearing a long robe with a gold sash across his chest. His head and his hair were white like wool, as white as snow. And his eyes were like flames of fire. His feet were like polished bronze refined in a furnace, and his voice thundered like mighty ocean waves. He held seven stars in his right hand, and a sharp two-edged sword came from his mouth. And his face was like the sun in all its brilliance.

> When I saw him, I fell at his feet as if I were dead. But he laid his right hand on me and said, "Don't be afraid! I am the First and the Last. I am the living one. I died, but look—I am alive forever and ever! And I hold the keys of death and the grave." (Revelation 1:12-18)

Zach's Final Thoughts

I love my city. I look around at its needs sometimes and get overwhelmed. Often I've thought to myself, "Really, what can I do? I have limited time, talent, and resources, and there is so much that needs to be done." It can be overwhelming, paralyzing.

I look at my friends who aren't seeking God—friends who don't see the point. To them, Christianity is just another tribe you can belong to. I long for them to see a God who can rebuild cities, illuminate the shadowed corners, and completely transform communities.

My fears shift to driving energy when I think about the untapped potential held by our small groups. I'm convinced that God will show himself—that God is already showing himself—in an unquestionable way through Christian communities. I'm pumped to see what happens when groups make the intentional decision that everything they do will be ignited by the mission of helping people far from God experience Christ. They will multiply with mission. They will serve with mission. They will engage in relationships with mission on their mind.

At culturalcows.com we will provide resources and continue the discussion. Join the conversation! Let's embrace the challenge to never settle for an adequate model. Let's offer permission to fail, listen to new voices, and experiment with new things—small group innovation in the name of God's kingdom. Because we believe that when people see Christian communities living under the mission of God, they will never have to ask, "Is this it?"

ACKNOWLEDGEMENTS

Last year, Austin and I grabbed some poster board and a marker and scribbled down some things we felt needed to be said about small groups. We hung them on the wall of my basement and began writing. Those thoughts would have stayed in the basement if it weren't for the following:

Our Families

I'm sure we drove our wives crazy with all our meetings and incessant requests of "read this," "what do you think about that?" and "can you edit this?" Through the whole process, our families were nonstop encouragers and willing sound boards. *From Couch to Community* would not exist if it weren't for our wives, Jaime Below and Chandra Maxheimer. That is a fact!

One Life Church

Austin and I feel very fortunate to be involved with the One Life network. It's amazing to be a part of a church whose leadership pushes its members to strive for more. One Life donated time, resources, encouragement, and leadership through this whole process. They found answers where we couldn't and connected us with helpful people we would have never found on our own. There was no way *From Couch to Community* would have happened without the support of One Life.

Check them out at **onelifechurch.org.**

Group Publishing

We also want to thank Group Publishing for all the great work they did to make this book possible. Special thanks to Amy Nappa and Bob D'Ambrosio for championing us along. We love being part of the Group team!

Check them out at **group.com.**

WORKS CITED

Chapter One

1. Lydia Saad, "U.S. Confidence in Organized Religion at Low Point," *Gallup*, 12 July 2012, http://www.gallup.com/poll/155690/Confidence-Organized-Religion-Low-Point.aspx.

2. David Kinnaman and Gabe Lyons, *unChristian: What a New Generation Really Thinks About Christianity...and Why It Matters*, (Grand Rapids, MI: Baker Books, 2007), 29-30.

3. David Kinnaman, *You Lost Me: Why Young Christians Are Leaving the Church and Rethinking Faith*, (Grand Rapids, MI: Baker Books, 2011), 79, 92-93.

4. Frank Newport., "In U.S., 77% Identify as Christian," *Gallup*, 24 December 2012, http://www.gallup.com/poll/159548/identify-christian.aspx.

Chapter Four

1. Colin Brown, ed. *The New International Dictionary of New Testament Theology*, vol. 1, s.v. "Disciple," (Grand Rapids, MI: Zondervan, 1975), 488.

Chapter Five

1. Tullian Tchividjian, "Focusing on Sin Never Works," *Relevant*, January/February 2012, 30.

Chapter Eleven

1. David Kinnaman and Aly Hawkins, "The Generation of Contrast: How Twenty- and Thirty-Somethings Are Changing the Shape of Christianity—For Better or Worse," *Relevant Magazine*, September/October 2011, 80-87.

2. Barna Group, "Barna Survey Examines Changes in Worldview Among Christians over the Past 13 Years," March 6, 2009, https://www.barna.org/barna-update/21-transformation/252-barna-survey-examines-changes-in-worldview-among-christians-over-the-past-13-years#.Uult7m2ivGV.

3. Barna Group, *The State of the Bible, 2013: A Study of U.S. Adults*, (Ventura, CA: Barna, 2013), 45, 62. http://www.americanbible.org/uploads/content/State%20of%20the%20Bible%20Report%202013.pdf.

4. Jean-Francois Lyotard, *The Postmodern Condition: A Report on Knowledge*, trans. Geoff Bennington and Brian Massumi, (Minneapolis, MN: University of Minnesota Press, 1984), xxiv.

5. Richard Middleton and Brian J. Walsh, *Truth Is Stranger Than It Used to Be: Biblical Faith in a Postmodern Age*, (Downers Grove, IL: InterVarsity Press), 28-42.

6. Engage International, "What Is Reveal?" http://engagechurches.com/reveal/what-is-reveal.

7. Greg L. Hawkins and Cally Parkinson, *Follow Me: What's Next for You?* (South Barrington, IL: Willow Creak Association, 2008), 114.

8. Erwin McManus, talk given at Catalyst Conference 2009, https://www.youtube.com/watch?v=REuTJeKPSvM.

Chapter Twelve

1. Seth Godin, *Tribes: We Need You to Lead Us,* (New York, NY: Penguin Group), 1-13.

2. Walter Isaacson, "In Search of the Real Bill Gates," *Time,* 13 January 1997, 44.

3. Roy Mack, "Pastor Appreciation, It's Not What You Think, Part 2," *Think On These Things* (blog), October 18, 2013, http://www.gracelives.com/pages/page.asp?page_id=289819.

4. Jay Pathak and David Runyon, *The Art of Neighboring: Building Genuine Relationships Right Outside Your Door,* (Grand Rapids, MI: Baker Books, 2012), 27-29.

Chapter Thirteen

1. Craig Groeschel, "The Strongest Link," Global Leadership Summit 2012, (Chicago, IL: Willow Creek Association, 2012), DVD.

Chapter Fifteen

1. Rodney Stark, *The Rise of Christianity: A Sociologist Reconsiders History,* (Princeton, NJ: Princeton University Press, 1996), 84.

Join the conversation at culturalcows.com.